SO, YOUR LOVED ONE IS TRANSGENDER. NOW, WHAT?

By:

Stephania M. Kanitsch

Foreword By Chris Alvarenga

"It matters not what someone is born, but what they grow to be."
— Albus Dumbledore

This book is devoted to my wonderful friends. Thanks for recognizing the person I have become. Thanks to the special people in my heart who encouraged me through the darkest of days and lifted my spirits. I am grateful for everyone who provided me the vision to give back through my writing. I would like to dedicate this to transgender individuals and their loved ones who are loving. We are paving a road to a better future.

TABLE OF CONTENTS

FOREWORD

I am delighted to write this foreword, not only because Stephania Kanitsch is my friend and business associate but also because I believe deeply in the educative value of her LGBTQ books & volunteer work. I also believe that families, friends, teachers, and therapists at every level can enrich and strengthen their LGBTQ relationships and teaching by learning practices presented in this book.

This inspired book is to Celebrate your Transgender loved one! For loved ones reaching out and reminding us to always say "I love you" to our LGBTQ children and people in our life.

Stephania's giving, touching others' lives, expanding the circle of the LGBTQ community concerns to include others, being authentic, and always open to receiving as well as giving. That's not just a fantasy. It's a good description of the amazing dedicated person she is.

Stephania untangles the wonderful, evolving language of sexuality and gender by providing explanations that are smart, engaging, and accessible for every kind of reader. You'll learn about:

- gender & sexual identity
- coming out
- raising LGBT children
- what a binary world means
- sex therapy
- ethical and training issues
- and more

"So, Your Loved One Is Transgender, Now What?" is making it easier to understand the LGBTQ+ identities. With first-hand experience and discussion and provides such a comprehensive read on terms and phrases in the queer and trans community."

Stephania has been a senior member of a local LGBTQ Nonprofit that she helped to start and worked with LGBTQ people and their friends and family for nearly a decade, and she has provided a resource with "So You're Transgender, Now What?" and "So, Your Loved One Is Transgender, Now What?" that pays such meticulous and thorough attention to the many nuances of sexuality and gender identity. Stephania Kanitsch's first book "So You're Transgender, Now What?" serves as a powerful tool for those that might be questioning their own identity, as well as for those seeking a deeper knowledge of the many, varied identities that exist in relation to their attractions, desires, and personal understandings of self.

"Stephania celebrates the wonderful, evolving language of sexuality and gender. By showcasing personal narratives and providing explanations, engaging, and accessible for every kind of reader, "So, Your Loved One Is Transgender, Now What?" provides a way for all of us to think about our unique experience and gives us just the help we need to communicate it to others."

Stephania Kanitsch lives in rural Texas and as a result of her kind heart and glowing spirit, has developed a strong bond with her local LGBTQ community where she's trusted, loved and admired for her voice in the LGBTQ community. Her insight and honest approach to LGBTQ education have helped kids and adults understand who they are.

This book is not overwhelming, it's not overly complicated, and it's not exhausting to read. It is under one hundred twenty pages of gender exploration, social justice, and practical resources. Stephania dissects gender using a comprehensive, non-binary toolkit, with a focus on making this subject easily accessible. All this to help you understand something that is so commonly misunderstood, but something we all think we get: gender.

Stephania Kanitsch is now working on her third book a comprehensive history of the LGBTQ community for young audiences of middle and high school youth to be released in the summer of 2020.

Royalties from this and other books from Stephania go back to the community.

Chris Alvarenga
Stephania Kanitsch's Friend & Business associate

INTRODUCTION

Your child comes out as transgender. The disclosure may be overwhelming and distressing. Your child senses the negativity projected and feels they cannot be themselves.

After a while, your child runs away. It can devastate a person. What will you do? As time passes, you hear nothing from your child. Your hope is they are not living on the streets.

Your phone rings one day. It is the police. They need you to identify your child. But this can be worse. You may have lost your child.

This scene is too familiar with the parents of transgender children. You loved them but could not get past your disappointment and embarrassment. And for what? Because you could not be the adult when your child needed you most. This may be harsh, but this is a reality for lots of transgender individuals.

Forty percent of juveniles on the streets are LGBTQ. This is significant considering only ≈ 4.2 percent of the population identifies as LGBTQ. Once they are on the streets, your child may go through hell. The sex industry recruitment is ongoing. The recruiters may use drugs to control your child. That is a tough existence. A greater percentage use drugs once on the street.

I knew I was transgender from an early age. My life was full of struggles from my gender identity. I tried to always have women's clothes to help reduce gender dysphoria.

In the early summer of 2013, my counselor started an LGBTQ group in the small town where we live. I met others like me at the first meeting. There were two other transgender women and one transgender man. The two transgender women had already started their transition. Upon seeing the happiness, they exhibited, I researched what it would take to become my true self.

My life included a larger than normal dysphoric feeling. I spent six months going back and forth with the reasons to start my transition, and the reasons not to.

Weighing this decision can exhaust a person You know you need to do this but also realize what it will do to your life.

I live in rural Texas. This weighed on my decision. I was unsure I would remain safe if I came out and transitioned. By the time I came out, my place of residence did not even figure into the equation.

You may ask yourself, what else weighed on my mind? The biggest thing was losing loved ones. How would my wife and her family react? How would my family react?

During the six months working toward my coming out, I researched everything I could find. I read a book on transitioning. I planned what I wanted to do in my transition and plotted it on a timeline and wrote a list of the positives and negatives and then supplied reasons for each item why it hampered what I would do.

I practiced on how I would come out to my wife. Though she accepted my dressing, I was unsure of how she would react when it became real. I was ready to lose her and be on the streets at this point. I knew I had to transition. For many transgender people, it becomes transitioning and living or not transitioning and taking your life because the gender dysphoria has gotten too bad to live with. My decision was to live.

Like most LGBTQ people, I was so scared prior to coming out. It was the toughest thing I have ever done. Do not let anyone convince you being gay, or transgender is a decision. People do not decide they want to lose family members, friends, and other loved ones. They do not decide things like this just to turn their life up-side-down. They do not put themselves in harm's way just to be their true selves. These are serious life-changing decisions.

I started hormones 40 days after coming out. I waited five months after starting hormones. My family lives a little over 1,000 miles from me. They received emails or Messenger PM.

I supplied the above, so you have an idea of what a transgender person goes through prior to coming out. Everyone's experience is different, but most of these feelings are the same. One of my future books will be concerning my life. I will say this; I write many experiences into this and other books. Experience makes for better reading and understanding.

I hope to shape minds and create a brighter future for transgender children. I hope for a future where coming out will be outdated. Can you express who you are without a part of society hating you for the garments you wear? It is difficult.

Lawmakers need to be affirming in the measures they pass. They should question bills introduced that deliver hate or discrimination.

Sounds impossible? It is not. It takes individuals to be honest and nonjudgmental. Educate yourself on why humans are transgender and gay.

Society may not make it to this level of acceptance, but any change is a start. Please use this book to supply your child or transgender loved one the love and support they need to make it through this demanding time.

Educate family members, friends, and neighbors. Advocate for those you care for. Be an ally. The transgender population is the most oppressed in the United States. This is unlikely to reverse soon. This places a burden on transgender individuals.

When you realize you may experience oppression, would you come out? Your child or a loved one may have come out because they had to. If your child asks for God to take them so they can be who they know they are, take notice. If you do not, you may lose them.

Transgender people experience life the same as everyone else. Why would people diminish that? To criticize someone who is different.

Throughout this book, I give insight into what can happen if you do not give the support and love they need. This in no way implies you are not supplying support. I offer it as a reference to help in your decision making and to help you supply help for those seeking guidance from you.

This book covers how to support your transgender loved one. Educating yourself is excellent. For more information on coming out and transitioning please refer to my first book "So, You're Transgender. Now What?"

One phrase used in this book is the deadname. A deadname is a previous name a transgender person had before changing it to more resemble their identity. This name is no longer around. It is a harsh phrase, but the transgender community uses it all the time. This allows you to become familiar with the phrase.

I do not have first-hand knowledge of what parents or other loved ones go through when their loved one says they are transgender. I believe by some of the experience with my coming out allows me to understand some of the feelings. This is not an easy proclamation for anyone involved.

Parents may feel like they are losing their children. This can be devastating. Therefore, initial responses should wait until they have a better understanding. The transgender person is only changing their outside appearance. Their personality and other traits may slightly change. You may see they are happier because of their body/mind congruence.

If you have feelings, you know you shouldn't try to resolve them. talk to your transgender loved one. Keep communication civil, but let them know you need to process the information you have just faced. Remember this, they have other people to face beside you with this announcement. This can cause anxiety and stress for the transgender person.

CHAPTER ONE: WHAT IS GENDER

Section One: Being Transgender

"I found power in accepting the truth of who I am. It may not be a truth that others can accept, but I cannot live any other way. How would it be to live a lie every minute of your life?"
— Alison Goodman, Eon: Dragoneye Reborn

This chapter gives details of what gender, transgender, and gender-expansive are. Though you may already know what being transgender is others who do not will find this information invaluable.

When you support your transgender loved one, you are providing them with a chance for a happier life.

When they came out, they are trusting those they have come out to with their secret. Return that trust with the love and care they ask for to help get through this. It is a priority for the future.

We misunderstand transgender people because the average person cannot imagine feeling their gender and sexual characteristics do not match. Most of the population most likely never think twice as to their gender.

When your sexual characteristics and gender do not match up, it can cause excessive stress and anxiety. A diagnosis of gender dysphoria is when stress and anxiety affect a person's mental health.

As a person who went through most of their life incongruent, gender dysphoria and underlying depression can have adverse reactions. If a person is transgender, it may be best for them to seek congruency as soon as possible. My childhood trauma and gender dysphoria have left me with depression that does not respond to treatment.

Allow your loved ones to enjoy their lives and achieve happiness.

Section Two: Gender Vs. Sexuality

Lesson number one: "Sexual orientation is who you go to bed with," he told Spack. "Gender identity is who you go to bed as."
— Amy Ellis Nutt, Becoming Nicole: The Transformation of an American Family

Society associates gender with primary sex characteristics. Others go further and claim sex characteristics and DNA determine gender. Neither of these assumptions is correct. There are differences that determine sex and gender.

What is the difference between gender identification and affectional orientation? Romance or affection is one part of a broader view of relationships.

Gender identity is who you know in your brain and comprehend you are. In most humans, these feelings are congruent with their birth sex. With transgender people, these two are not congruent. This can cause extreme stress. Affectional orientation pertains to who you feel comfortable and attracted to, be it romantically or sexually.

Gender expression is often used to signify a person's day-to-day expression of themselves. It may not match their gender identity. Gender expression is a person's dress, hair, accessories they adopt to communicate their identity. A person's gender identity and gender expression may not be equal. One day they may express their gender. The next day they may express androgynous. Their gender identity remains the same. Only their expression varies. Over time, their identity may evolve. This is because of a better understanding of who they are. Most individuals gender stays stable throughout life.

Most people's DNA matches what science informs them is correct for their primary sex characteristics. Females have XX chromosomes and males XY. But wait! A person's chromosomes determine the sex of the individual, not the gender. But chromosomes do not always decide sex characteristics either. There are variations where females' DNA is XY chromosomes and males XX chromosomes. Some individuals may have one X chromosome. There may be three or more letters together. Human chromosome combinations vary. Thus, chromosomes do not always determine sex.

"Women have female parts and men have male parts." Really? Men may get gynecomastia which can cause their breast tissue to develop. If they take anti-androgens for a medical issue, they may cause gynecomastia. Does that mean they are part women? No. When a female has breast cancer and has their breasts removed does that make them a man? No.

Society determines a person's sex by their primary sex characteristics. We realize gender in our brains. Most people's sense of their gender matches their primary sex characteristics.

If they do not transition, they may not achieve the happiness they deserve. They are inhibiting their ability to show their identity. They may never attain happiness if they fear expressing their true feelings, views, and wishes. They only have one life. Let them enjoy it.

A large portion of society fears the unknown. Educate yourself and others. It is necessary and helps them. By acknowledging who they are you offer them the strength to be their true selves.

Six most common DNA karyotypes (These are the karyotypes that do not result in the fetus's death)	
X	1 in 2,000 to 1 in 5,000 people (Turner's Syndrome)
XX	Most common female karyotype
XXY	1 in 500 to 1 in 1,000 people (Klinefelter's Syndrome)
XY	Most common male karyotype
XYY	1 in 1,000 people
XXXY	1 in 18,000 to 1 in 50,000 births

Section Three: Definition of Transgender?

"I've always been transgender, and I always will be. Having said that, my spirit is feminine. If you had to divide humanity into two groups, I would sit with the women."
— Anohni

Transgender is when a person's gender identity and primary sex characteristics do not match. This incongruence creates issues, including gender dysphoria. Even though a person realizes they are transgender, they may not transition. Negative stereotypes against the transgender community do not help in their pursuit of happiness. When people repeat stereotypes, it can destroy the class of people they direct them at.

The term transgender is an umbrella term for anyone who identifies as a gender outside the gender binary. There are those who are the gender binary (trans male or trans females), gender fluid, non-binary, bigender, and gender non-conforming among many others. All genders are legitimate. There are transgender individuals who may not label their gender. Most dislike living within a world of labels.

Intersex is when an individual is born with ambiguous genitalia, among other differences. This is not the same as being transgender. Intersex people may identify as transgender if their genitalia were "altered" after birth. The practice of "altering" the genitalia is mutilation. These surgeries at birth need to cease. Allow intersex people the opportunity to select their preferred primary sex characteristics and gender.

When label people and put them into specific boxes, there will continue to be oppression for those who in smaller populations.

Section Four: You Cannot Change Genders

"Terror doesn't change people from gay to straight. It just hurts innocent people."
— DaShanne Stokes

Some organizations say gender and sexuality can be changed. This is not possible. Transgender people are born this way. A person's gender is unchangeable. The same holds for their sexuality.

Reparative therapy (conversion therapy aka ex-gay therapy) Religious and mental health people claim reparative therapy can alter a person's gender and/or sexuality. Nothing needs to change. Second, it does not work. Third, this may be risky for an individual's mental health condition.

Legitimate national organizations stand by their statements stating reparative therapy is ineffective and unethical. Mental health issues can become worse, including becoming psychotic.

Please do not consider this barbaric therapy. There are over 16 states with laws restricting this therapy for anyone under 18. Believe what these organizations say. A person's gender cannot change and can do permanent harm to an individual's mental health status.

I have seen first-hand the damage reparative therapy can do.

In the past, they used to perform lobotomies, electric shock, and other barbaric therapies. If you have considered doing this, please reconsider.

Section Five: Everyone Has a Gender Identity

Gender is really varied and complicated and sort of infinitely individualistic.
— Susan Faludi

Many people never give a second thought to their gender. Transgender people do because their sex characteristics and gender are incongruent.

Most children know their gender by six years old. Some transgender people's realization may not be as strong until later in life. Even those whose realization comes later say they knew something was not right. My awareness came at three or four years old. I knew at 12 years old what it was.

Though there is a correlation between assumed gender and sex, many factors relate to a person's gender. Recent research shows transgender people have a part of the brain which provides a sense of gender having a shape the same as a cisgender person of that gender.

We should not gender articles such as crafts, toys, clothes, and others. No one person is the same as another. A person's interest can cross over between males and females. By gendering items, society is announcing these items or crafts are for a specific gender. If you're a male and want to knit, knit. Don't let society's labeling of everything keep you from doing something you love.

CHAPTER TWO: TRANSGENDER CHILDREN <10 YEARS OLD

Section One: Transgender Children < 10 yrs. old

"It's easy to fictionalize an issue when you're not aware of the many ways in which you are privileged by it."
—*Kate Bornstein, Gender Outlaws: The Next Generation*

What will you do if your child comes up and says. "mommy, I'm not a girl, I'm a boy" or "mommy, I'm not a boy, I'm a girl?" Emotions run wild. There can be heartache and pain. Use this time to review your beliefs, life, and your child. Don't ignore your beliefs, make sure you address them. Supply them love and understanding. It is a challenge for parents. Confusion can terrify your child.

Educating yourself is essential. This provides for an easier journey for everyone involved. The more you understand, the easier it will be to accept their journey. The older your child is, the tougher for them to come out and face society. If they announce they are another gender, support them. Their mental health and gender dysphoria can suffer from not being open to their identity.

Young transgender kids can get gender dysphoria the same as older people. Gender dysphoria starts with the stress and anxiety of not being congruent. Embrace your child when you see these behaviors from them. This is essential to their future.

In the next few sections, we will deal with what a young child may encounter. These sections offer information on how to determine if they may be transgender. There is no test or any other way to know for sure, but you can be confident they are. They came out because you are their parent and they trust you. Show that trust by offering the best care possible. Help them develop into a happy adolescent and adult. Provide them a chance at an enjoyable life. All children deserve that chance.

Provide counseling. Therapists are an asset, particularly gender therapists.

Young children are resilient but have their limits. The necessity to express their identity can be significant.

Section Two: They Said What?

"Nothing prepares the parent of a transgender child, and nothing prepares that child. For me, that's the good news: no rule book."
— Nancy Moore

Words you hope to never hear; "You know I'm not a boy, I'm a girl" or "you know I'm not a girl, I'm a boy." Most people know what the current mood is surrounding the transgender community. Some parents may accept their child being transgender but resent society for making it unsafe for them to exist. No one desires to have their child tormented and to go through a tumultuous childhood.

Even when they do not transition your child's life may still be rough. Gender dysphoria can be debilitating. Trying to wade through life with an incongruent body is rough. Puberty can make it even more so. Once puberty starts, their body changes in ways they would rather it didn't. Their gender dysphoria can grow worse. You believe your child is "normal," but what is normal? Uniqueness is the wonderful quality everyone has. There is no "normal." Children are individuals, and they are unique. Embrace this uniqueness. Transgender people have something special very few people get to realize. Their authenticity.

My knowledge is limited in what a transgender loved one goes through. Their loved ones' first response can be negative. Try to avoid instant reactions to their announcement. An initial negative reaction can hurt your loved one and any rapport you have with them. Make sure you have time to sit down by yourself and reflect on what they have told you before responding. Initial responses may not be your true feelings. Make certain before proceeding with further conversations, you have resolved any bad feelings.

This is not a phase. Give them a positive experience they will thank you for. If you deal with it negatively by not providing them love and support, it can affect their future. If it is a phase, they will be grateful for the love you have shown them.

It is tougher for older children to come out. They may take months or years to test the waters regarding their parent's acceptance. They need to love themselves first. It's a part of being able to accept your identity. Negativity towards transgender and/or LGB individuals makes it harder to reveal this.

The positive news is the present climate for transgender individuals is better than the past. The community and society are heading in the right direction. Our future looks brighter for transgender people, but there is still a lot of work to accomplish.

Some religions believe being transgender is against God's word. We will not engage in that discussion. If you have these beliefs, you need to reevaluate your view. If they believe they may go to hell, they may see they cannot be their true selves. This may lead them to hurt themselves. Provide positive support. Provide them a chance to flourish or you may lose them.

By reading this book you have taken a positive step forward for your child. I'm grateful for your choice. I hope you walk away from this book with a clearer understanding. No one book can offer all the information you may want. No two transitions are alike. Experiences are as individual as people are.

It is a tough journey for everyone. Anxiety, exhilaration, grief and other emotions are common. Children go through these same emotions. Remember this, it is ano ones fault, it is biology.

Section Three: How do They Know so Young?

"If people are going to judge me without fully understanding the content of my character, then their opinion just isn't worth it."
— Jazz Jennings

Ask your young cisgender child who they are. They will tell you what gender they are. I realized at three or four years old. I was unclear what I felt but I knew there was something different. This can be frightening to a young person. They may have shame or guilt because of society's negativity. It will become their secret to keep. Even for small children, it can lead to anxiety and depression.

How do I recognize they are transgender? Is it a phase? There is no clear way to tell. There are three signs which may offer a better understanding.

Most children understand what their gender is no later than six years old. There are exceptions. They know mom and dad and understand who their sisters and brothers are. They can separate males from females. From a young age, the media displays the gender binary. This is how they know their gender so young. They learn through their interaction with those around them and from media. (films, tv, their play computer)

They may also recognize from interaction with play friends, toys and other items which society has put a gender to.

Three signs they may be transgender:

•—**Persistent:** Saying they are not the gender the doctor claimed them to be. This persistence can emerge in many forms. When they state who they are, announcing "Put me back in mommy's tummy so I can come back right" or praying to God to take them to heaven.

•—**Consistent:** Consistency in their message to the family regarding their gender. If they play with the other gender's toys or the other gender.

•—**Insistent:** Insistent about who they are and the gender they are.

Most children who come out at an early age exhibit at least one of these three signs. It is typical for them to exhibit all three. Parents need to understand what their child is telling them. The more parents avoid this, the more insistent they can become. Ignoring or disciplining them will not stop them from being transgender. You cannot change who they are. Would a person seek to change their cisgender child to transgender?

They may play with the other gender's toys. They may be a feminine male or masculine female. This could be a signal they may be transgender.

Trust what they are saying. This is not something anyone chooses. Your child is not trying to embarrass or harm you. Give them the same respect. Help them by welcoming the new person they are growing into.

Section Four: Not a Choice

"She did not talk about choices because being transgender is not a choice. Transgender people don't cross over and live as the other gender. They aren't exploring different sides. They are not changing their minds or trying to 'pass.' They are, and always have been, the other gender. They have never felt aligned with the gender assigned at birth according to anatomy or genes." "The only real choice is whether to live as their true selves or live a lie. For many, this decision is a matter of life and death."
— *Deborah L. Davis Ph.D., Laugh, Cry, Live*

Skin color and ethnicity are not an alterable trait. Neither is being transgender. I had hoped I would not have to come out, but now that I'm out I wouldn't have it any other way. If someone asked me to take a pink pill to be a female or a blue pill to be male, I would request the pink pill. This is who I am.

It is fortunate transgender people can transform their bodies into their correct gender through medical and surgical techniques.

Few transgender people revert to their old gender. Being transgender is easier than it was 50 years ago but is still tough. Past generations of transgender people went through their transition in private. There are still some who do this. Once they find congruency, they start a new life. Transitioning nowadays does not require giving up your past. They may move to a more accepting locale, but do not leave behind their prior life.

Nobody wishes to lose family and friends. Being genuine shouldn't put a target on your back. Everyone should have an enjoyable and productive life. Support them through this and do not diminish their ability to be themselves.

Section Five: Patience

"It's not how you start that's important, but how you finish!"
— Jim George

Having patience can be hard during these times. Gather your senses and resolve to educate yourself on what being transgender is. Your loved one may be new to this. Their expression of their identity may be only at home to start. Give them the safety to do this. Let them navigate their course through this journey. It is their journey. Do not impede it. They may prefer to express their identity everywhere except school or they may transition in public.

Remember trust? Keep it by allowing them to take the lead. This is difficult for everyone. Be prepared for the unexpected. No two transitions are alike. Your child may want to wear tights, get their ears pierced, and other ways of expressing their gender. If they are a transgender male, they may prefer boys' shoes and clothes. Let them take the lead in their style.

As they get closer to puberty, make certain you get educated on the effects of puberty blockers and why they are essential for your child. This is an important decision. If they do not start on puberty blockers, their puberty will advance forward as their assigned sex at birth (ASAB). For many transgender people, going through puberty and experiencing the wrong puberty can devastate them.

Why are puberty blockers important? Puberty blockers give them a chance to stop their puberty until they are mature enough to decide on hormones (HRT hormone replacement therapy). Blockers pause their puberty to allow them to mature.

The hormones allow for their secondary sex characteristics to progress as their real gender. This is essential for their identity.

Section Six: Avoid Stereotypes

"When the Majority of jokes made at the expense of trans people center on 'men wearing dresses' or 'men who want their penises cut off' that is not transphobia- it is trans-misogyny. When the majority of violence and sexual assaults committed against trans people is directed at trans women, that is not transphobia- it is trans-misogyny."
— Julia Serano, Whipping Girl: A Transsexual Woman on Sexism and the Scapegoating of Femininity

Stereotypes are rampant in oppressed communities. Stereotypes are a part of the cycle of oppression. Though there are positive and negative stereotypes I have never heard a positive stereotype. There are many negative stereotypes. Learn what they are. You may believe what you are saying is acceptable. If you are unsure, ask. Asking is better than saying something demeaning. Make sure what you say is respectable.

Common stereotypes:

•—Transgender people believe that they are "born in the wrong body."
Transgender individuals are in the bodies they were born with. Their primary sex characteristics do not match the gender they know. As children, they may say they were born in the wrong body to say their feelings.

•—Transgender people have confusion or are trying to fool others.
Why would they want to trick others? So they can get hassled, discriminated against, and even lose their lives? They are going against societal norms. No one wishes to have someone assault them. Transgender people do not have confusion over their gender. They may have confusion at first of what they are feeling.

•—Transitioning is as simple as one surgery.
When a person transitions it involves multiple activities. There is an assortment of ways to become congruent with their bodies. Their transition requires relearning to walk, talk, act, and express as their new identity. They may end up with a unique style and wardrobe. Few transgender people get "the surgery" because of costs and risks. To relieve extreme gender dysphoria, they may elect for the surgery.

•—Children are not mature enough to know their gender identity.
Read the ***How Does My Child Know so Young?*** chapter. Most children know their gender by six years old.

•—There is an association between sexual orientation and gender identity.
See the chapter titled ***Gender Identity vs. Affectional Orientation*** Hint: There is a relationship between them, just not what most people think.

•—Transgender people go through medical transition.
There are around five steps to a "complete transition." Because your child comes out as transgender does not mean they will transition. They may only accomplish a social transition. When a transgender person does not take hormones or get surgeries, their transition is only social. Each individual person chooses what they will finish for their congruence. What they do or don't do does not make them any less transgender.

•—Transgender people have mental health problems.
The state of being transgender does not cause mental health problems. Gender dysphoria is a diagnosis. Gender dysphoria comes from internal and external sources of being transgender. Transgender people use a larger percentage of mental healthcare.

There are a few reasons for this. The depression rate for transgender people is more than for cisgender persons. Harassment and bullying can trigger depression.

Changing your name/gender, starting hormones, or to get surgeries may require authorization through healthcare professionals. If a transgender person feels they cannot or may not become their authentic self, they may have anxiety and stress, leading to mental health complications. They may use a mental health expert to help them discover who they are.

•—Drag queens and kings are transgender.
Dressing up to perform as the opposite gender does not make a person transgender. There are more drag performers coming out as transgender. They may believe it to be safer and more accepting now.

There are many more stereotypes beyond these.

Section Seven: Let Them Express Their Gender

"To parents who find a child's disclosure about sexual or gender identity challenging, I always urge what I'd call 'moderated' honesty. If you can't say 'I love you', then say something like, 'I'm going to need some time to digest this news.' Buy time this way. And then think."
— Steven Petrow

Your loved one may not feel they are any one gender. They may want to figure out where they fit on the gender spectrum. Let them. There is an endless number of genders. They may be gender-expansive (gender non-conforming GNC). Your child may move around genders over the years. They are discovering themselves. This becomes clearer when they start puberty. They will want to fit into society.

Children under 10 may shift through the gender spectrum if they are unclear who they are. They learn through discovery. With transgender children, the discovery of themselves is a lot more open and visual.

Their style may forever change. For transgender people who come out later in life, they may need to try styles that may not fit their age.

If your child is transgender, it can be a challenge, but have fun with it. Take them shopping for clothes or toys.

Section Eight: Your Child's Transition

"Refuse to be your child's first bully."
— Anonymous

Children under 10 years old go through a social transition. Before puberty begins, get educated on their future. This makes any future choices easier. A social transition is changing their clothing, accessories, shoes, and other things appropriate for their gender.

Transitioning can involve many things or nothing at all. Let your child take the lead on what they want to do. If you believe a choice of theirs is wrong, advise them on why it's wrong. Your new daughter may wish to wear dresses, tights, or grow her hair longer or new son may want to wear boy's clothes and a short haircut. Your new daughter has always been your daughter and your new son has always been your son.

There are other actions that they can accomplish but may require the parent's approval, such as getting their ears pierced. Bracelets, necklaces and various other accessories may help, too.

Upon onset of puberty, they may go back to their prior gender. This does not mean they are no longer transgender. Their comfort and security may prove better identifying as the gender of their birth sex. Once they reach puberty and are still expressing their correct gender, they are most likely transgender.

You may hear otherwise, but children under 16 do not start hormones. There are exceptions. Attitudes regarding this are changing. Puberty blockers are not hormones. They stop puberty by blocking the body from making estrogen or testosterone until the adolescent is mature enough to recognize what hormone replacement therapy does and the bodily changes it produces. If they start puberty early you and your child may face this decision earlier.

CHAPTER THREE: YOUR TRANSGENDER CHILD >10-18

Section One: Adolescence is Tough

"Everybody's got a past," he said. "That doesn't mean you can't have a future."
— Meredith Russo, If I Was Your Girl

Everyone's teen years can tumultuous, even for a straight cisgender person. For transgender teens who have come out, and even those who haven't, it can be devastating.

It is vital to listen to what your child is saying. They are vulnerable during this time. The attempted suicide rate for transgender people is 41 percent. They make most attempts before 25 years old. (92 percent) [1] Suicide is not the only risk. In order for your child to be their true identity, they may run away. The streets are unsafe. Transgender and LGBTQ individuals are at a greater risk of violence when on the street. Forty percent of youth on the streets are LGBTQ. Of those, 46 percent are there because their families rejected them. An astonishing 67 percent of transgender youths are in the sex trade. [2] This is because of higher rates of intolerance, violence and economic instability compared to their peers. Many enter the sex industry just to survive.

Within 48 hours of leaving home, the sex trade will recruit one in three youths. Once in the sex trades, it's tough to get out. They can end up being trafficked.

When your child comes out as transgender, they may be unsure of where they fit on the gender spectrum. They may want to take their time for safety reasons. There are those who may transition slower than others. This does not diminish their identity.

Provide them counseling so they have an unbiased person to communicate with. If they are uncertain of their feelings, use a gender therapist, where workable. Gender therapists have more knowledge of the transition process and can better manage your child in their journey.

I am not saying you will lose your child. The need to be yourself is powerful enough to lead your loved one to do things they otherwise would not.

Section Two: Why are They Just Coming Out

"A transgender child comes out when they feel comfortable or need to. This does not mean they just turned transgender at 16. They were always transgender."
— *Stephania Kanitsch*

There are many reasons your child may not have come out to at a younger age. Safety is the main reason for waiting. Some transgender individuals are uncertain where they fit in. When they compare themselves with other children, they recognize something is different but may not understand what. Children with cell phones are better able to understand what they are feeling by searching. Even if their identity is something they have learned about online, it is important to offer them counseling to help them through this discovery. Children may come out earlier because this information is at their fingertips.

Your child may come out because they have figured out their feelings and what they equate to. There are some transgender people whose realization comes later in life. The strength of these feelings may determine when they know who they are.

They may keep this secret their whole life. This makes them no less transgender. It means society's acceptance of transgender people may not be adequate for them to come out. Everyone wants others to see them as the person they are.

Section Three: Keep Their Secret

"But you can only lie about who you are for so long without going crazy."
— *Ellen Wittlinger, Parrotfish*

It is essential parents do not out their transgender child. They will open to people they feel safe around. When they do not desire to be out as transgender outside of your home, offer this security for them. They know better how their friends will react. An individual will not tell someone a secret unless they have trust in who they are telling. If the parents' show a negative reaction to LGBTQ people, and the environment is adverse towards LGBTQ people, they may see it as risky coming out.

An individual comes out once. This is their chance to announce to people who they are. Help make it a wonderful memory for them. There is only this one time to offer them the love they need. If your response is negative, you will not get a do-over. They will remember your response, positive and negative, and it can influence their future relationship with you. They may show you the same trust in the future. Don't lose their trust in you. This is a huge step for everybody. Start off on the right foot.

Forty or more years ago, you could lose your life for being transgender. You still can. In the past, many started their life over by disappearing and going through their transition. They would lose families and friends to be their true selves. It was essential for their survival. Your child may not see another way to be themselves so they may disappear, and you may never see them again. Do not let this happen.

Section Four: Like-Minded People

"Sorry to disappoint you, parents – but when your kids come out as gay, bi or
transgender, it is not about you."
— Christina Engela, Fearotica: An Anthology of Erotic Horror

It will become clear that finding like-minded individuals will help in relieving stress and as a good information source. Communication becomes crucial to negotiate any obstacles you and your child will experience. Find like-minded people going through the same struggle. Interact with them. Their input can become invaluable.

Your child should find help through other transgender children. They can share experiences. If the other child is further along in their transition, they can offer valuable knowledge for your child which may not be unavailable anywhere else.

If you are in a rural area, it may be tougher to locate these like-minded individuals. There are many groups on Facebook that cater to the exclusive needs of the transgender person and their loved one. Some groups may not allow children under 18 to become members and take part.

Support groups are available for parents of transgender loved ones. There is a hidden group on Facebook called Mama Bears. They assess you for the other members' security. It is a hidden group supplying extra security.

If you live in or near a larger city, it should be easier to find someone to talk with. When there is a person available who is going through the same thing it can make their journey less stressful.

Try to offer the same help to others you received.

Transgender people who go stealth (living as their gender identity without identifying as transgender) can still give back. They supported you. Support others in need. If your family wishes to stay stealth, you can give back without being out to others.

Section Five: Healthcare Support

"Being transgender isn't a medical transition. It's a process of learning to love yourself for who you are."
— Jazz Jennings

Throughout your child's transition, therapy is advisable. If they have come out to you but remain unsure of their identity, it would be a good idea to offer them therapy, preferably from a gender therapist. If they continue on their journey after socially transitioning, they will need emotional and medical help for most medical and surgical interventions.

Many transgender individuals, even those under 18 get gender dysphoria. If your child has gender dysphoria, they will need help to resolve it.

When selecting mental health and endocrinologist professionals for your adolescent, ask if they have had transgender clients in the past. Familiarity with adolescents helps. Ask if they know what the WPATH Standards of Care are and if they adhere to them. By adhering to these standards your adolescent should get the proper care.

Prior to starting puberty blockers or hormones, your child needs to see a mental health professional. Endocrinologists will require your child is transgender before prescribing them. They will require your child has seen a mental health professional ensure they are transgender.

If your endocrinologist uses the WPATH Standards of Care for transgender individuals, it will require them to see a therapist get a letter stating they are ready and recognize the effects of any medical intervention. Most endocrinologists require the patient to understand the effects of hormones are not reversible.

There is no proof puberty blockers affect the body. Even though there is no research on long-term harm from puberty blockers, make certain your transgender child sees a pediatric endocrinologist often after starting them. Regular check-ups ensure they are progressing without complications. There are beliefs puberty blockers can cause issues with bone growth.

The timely treatment of puberty blockers may help to resolve their gender dysphoria.

For transgender girls, puberty blockers will inhibit the growth of their penis. This may influence their capability to have adequate tissue if they want gender confirmation surgery (GCS). GCS is surgery which alters their genitalia to the gender they are. There are procedures that take tissue from other parts of the body for GCS.

Hormone changes are permanent. Few, if any of the changes reverse. There is no way to determine what changes may reverse once they stop hormones. Both mental health and medical professionals want the adolescent to understand what these changes are.

If your loved one desires to have children, they will need to bank their sperm or eggs. Testosterone blockers and estrogen render transgender females infertile. Once on testosterone, transgender males may not conceive. Discussions and decisions should be made before starting hormones.

Therefore there are requirements for the adolescent to be mature so they make informed decisions. After certain steps in their transition, the effects are not reversible. No conclusive studies show that when a transgender male ends testosterone, they can conceive again. These choices have life-changing outcomes.

The WPATH Standards exist as a gatekeeper. Most professionals follow these standards with minors. When they assess minors, health experts should make certain the four following statements are true:

1. — The adolescent has established a long-lasting and strong sequence of gender nonconformity or gender dysphoria (whether concealed or expressed);
2. — Gender dysphoria appeared or exacerbated with puberty; (this is not true with a good deal of healthcare professionals. There are transgender individuals who never exhibit gender dysphoria)
3. — Discuss any co-existing mental, medical, or social issues that could prevent treatment (e.g., that may compromise treatment adherence). This encompasses the adolescent's condition and functioning are solid enough to establish treatment;
4. — The adolescent has provided informed consent and if the adolescent has not attained the age of medical consent, the parents or guardians consented to the procedure(s) and remain engaged in aiding the adolescent throughout their treatment. [3] There are transgender individuals who have had GCS prior to age 18. These are extraordinary situations. It is best for those affected to have the wisdom of what GCS entails. This is crucial if your child aims to get GCS right after they turn 18.

Gender dysphoria is not always a requirement. There are transgender people who do not exhibit gender dysphoria. Your support is crucial to their future.

Section Six: Education is Crucial

Education is society's most valuable asset. It provides insight, intellect, can cut discriminations, and further informs people. If you love your child, educating others is of utmost importance. Your understanding of the why's, how's, and other topics helps the relationship you have with them.

Try to recognize the pressures your loved one is dealing with. Help them through the rough spots. The suicide attempt rate for transgender adults is 41 percent. There is minimal research concerning the transgender population. Research for transgender people under 18 is even more scarce. More research is being performed all the time. The rate of suicide attempts drops when they receive love, encouragement, and affirmation. Recent research shows transgender males under 18 have a greater rate of suicide attempts than transgender females.

Transgender people have always existed. They are just now in people's radars because of attacks from government and religious entities.

There are varied factors comprising transitions. There are five steps to transitioning. Everyone is unique and each person's transition is unique. They may accomplish all the steps or none. They may wish to only finish their social transition.

There may be reasons for not starting or finishing some steps. This may be because of medical complications. Where they live can influence their capability to transition. Some localities are easier to come out in. Most large metropolitan areas are accepting of transgender individuals, whereby many rural areas are not.

They are no less transgender if they do not transition.

For more guidance on their transitioning read my first book, "So You're Transgender. Now, What?". There are various steps to transitioning which require letters from therapists and/or medical doctors. These letters show they are ready for hormones, surgeries, and other interventions.

Section Seven: Affirmation

"It's not just a pronoun… No. It's not. Trust me, some of the smallest things can make a world of difference…"
— Anonymous

Affirmation is providing emotional support and encouragement. We accomplish this through education, acceptance of their identity, and support for their transition. When you affirm who your child is it sends a powerful message of the love, you have for them.

Addressing your loved one with the correct pronouns and their selected name is affirming. The ability to remember and use the correct pronouns is tough but becomes easier as time goes on. If a person acknowledges a transgender person using incorrect pronouns on purpose, it is harmful. When someone uses the incorrect pronouns, they are denying the person's identity. If you find it hard using the correct pronouns, address them by their chosen name. This may make it tough to remember but is not malicious. You will see it gets easier as time goes on.

Once they have chosen their new name, use it. If they have not chosen a name yet, ask if you can help. This shows you care.

It's all right to grieve the loss of the person they were. This is tough for everyone involved. You are not giving up the person you love. They are still the same person on the inside. Only their outside is changing. They are correcting their identity, and you are the one transitioning by interacting with the new person they are becoming.

Discuss your child's emotions with them and what they desire to get out of their transition. Show your interest in their success in becoming their authentic selves.

Listen closely to what your child is telling you. Inquire as to their emotions throughout this journey. Keep communications open throughout their transition. It is essential to know their desires, what they are going through, and show your love for them.

Be their best ally. Show concern for other transgender people. Go to Pride. Show your pride in them and remain by their side. They need you in their life right now. Get involved in advocacy to offer the transgender community a brighter future. The transgender community has seen progress in recent years but they lost ground since 2016. The transgender community needs as many people as possible to assist them in achieving their equality.

Be prepared to deal with any challenging conversations. The dialog may turn to sex or sexuality. Be ready! There are many delicate issues you and your child will face. If you're not confident in your answer, let them know you will get back to them.

Do not out them. If they are not out to other relatives, seek your child's approval to inform others. This provides for more open family gatherings. If gatherings involve gift-giving, make clear relatives give presents matching the transgender person's new identity. Receiving a card or present addressed with their deadname or old pronouns is hurtful.

Section Eight: Counseling

"Transpeople lose a number of things when we transition. We can lose family, friends, jobs, children, lovers, and money. But the most difficult thing for me to lose has been veracity. I was already used to not being real, but now I don't even seem to be trustworthy. I'm not a reliable reporter about my sex or my gender or even my own name; I cannot be trusted to be my own expert. In each of those querying moments, what I am being asked for detail so someone else can make the final decision—am I real yet?"
— S. Bear Bergman

The transition process is a huge undertaking for everyone. Everyone involved should seek qualified counseling. Give your transgender child the courtesy to keep their counseling conversations private. Your child may prefer to discuss matters with their counselor they may not otherwise discuss.

Though you may wish to use a gender therapist for your child, you may also require a family therapist to help the family through this time.

By seeking counseling, you are showing you care for them and their result even if you are not happy with their adventure. Give yourself space to maneuver this.

If they have gender dysphoria, they should see a counselor for help to resolve it. If they are out to you but uncertain of what is causing their confusion, a counselor can help sort through that.

Work through everyone's concerns. Their personality will remain the same, except they will be much happier. When they achieve their congruency, it is inspiring.

Section Nine: Puberty Blockers

"It's not my appearance that defines me, but my heart and soul."
— Anonymous

Allow your young teen the chance to delay their puberty. This makes their life brighter. If you allow them to use puberty blockers, they will delay their secondary sex characteristics from developing. This means the voice of those born male at birth will not drop, their voice box will not bulge from their neck, among other assorted things. It means your assigned female loved one will not develop breasts, begin their period, among other changes.

There are reasons your child should take puberty blockers. It offers them time to learn what the effects of the hormones are, known as cross-sex hormones, before starting them. As stated above the blockers block the secondary sex characteristics from starting. If a transgender child goes through puberty without taking puberty blockers, it can be tougher to "pass" when they start hormones. For transgender people, going through puberty as the wrong sex can cause severe gender dysphoria. If they elect not to transition, they can stop the blockers and continue through their full puberty.

Transgender males who may not take puberty blockers may require top surgery to have their breasts removed and rebuild their nipples. Transgender women may require laser hair removal if their beard has started. To fit in better, they will need to change their voice. By allowing them the comfort of taking puberty blockers, the puberty process could have been easier.

Research into the effects of puberty blockers on an adolescent's body is new. There are several effects that may occur. Puberty blockers can produce bone thinning. Reducing estrogen levels in those assigned female at birth can bring on temporary osteopenia (like menopause when amounts of estrogen fall). For individuals assigned female at birth, a 2009 study found it lessened their bone density but came back within 10 years after stopping blockers. [4] There was a study of men with prostate cancer in 2005 that discovered taking GnRH analog medications (i.e. puberty blockers) can put them at a greater risk of bone fractures. [4] There are questions whether puberty blockers reduce the growth of the brain in adolescents. Problems may occur with the size of the penis of a transgender girl and whether it will be large enough to make the vaginal cavity if they desire surgery.

They designed puberty blockers for children who started puberty early. Puberty blockers use for transgender children is an off-label usage. There is not adequate research to substantiate it limits the growth of the brain.

Section Ten: Schools! Know Ahead of Time

"bathroom: (n.) where Americans go to argue about gender while the country
goes down the toilet."
— Sol Luckman, The Angel's Dictionary

Prior to your transgender child starting in school make sure you know their policies for transgender children. Many school districts already have in place policies addressing transgender individual's restroom and locker room usage. They may already have policies in place on addressing transgender students by their correct names and pronouns. This is essential to reducing stress for your child while they are attending school.

School districts in smaller municipalities may not have discussed or do not have existing transgender student policies. If their district has not had a transgender student yet, they may not have a plan. Make certain you communicate with the superintendent and principal regarding your child. It is essential your child understands what they will encounter on their first day of school. Bring it up at a school board meeting. To deal with this, districts may dictate students to use the nurse's restroom. This is not appropriate. This is your moment to advocate for your child.

Discrimination is when they restrict transgender individuals from using the restroom of their gender. It is not for anybody's security. Your child will be at a higher risk of being bullied, harassed, and even injured by using the restroom that conforms to their assigned sex at birth. There is no evidence a transgender person has assaulted another person while using the restroom. It is tough enough coming out as transgender. It is even harder using the restroom conforming to their gender identity.

There are transgender people who hold their urine until they arrive at a restroom accepting of their gender. Your child may hold their urine from the moment they leave for school in the morning until they get home later in the afternoon. This can lead to kidney complications and bladder infections.

Many people cannot afford to move to an affirming school district, but it will make a substantial difference in their child's life.

Section Eleven: Not a Fad

"People didn't start coming out as transgender after Caitlyn Jenner as a fad. They came out because she inspired them to be brave enough to be themselves."
— Anonymous

Children who are gender-variant in their earlier life have a greater chance of being transgender once they start puberty This is not a trend. Perceiving it as a fad diminishes their identity.

There are organizations and people who believe being transgender is a fad. They say there is a new diagnosis of Rapid Onset Gender Dysphoria (ROGD). This is not a DSM diagnosis, even though it may sound like one. This phrase first appeared in July 2016 in three separate blogs. It's used to explain to parents why children were coming out as transgender, and the influence transgender children have on those they interact with. There is no such thing as ROGD. It is another way of denying transgender people exist.

There are risks, hostility, and harassment. It may appear to be a trend to others but is far from that. Violence and hate are worse.

The teen years are tough for everybody. They are coming of age but are still under their parent's supervision. They started puberty. Puberty alone can create chaos. Puberty for transgender people is even harder. Their body is changing in ways which are not acceptable for their gender. This makes it tougher to understand what these feelings are. But oppression and stereotypes regarding transgender people are real. Listen to what they reveal to you. Let it sink in before reacting. Learn what transgender is. Most transition in time. The negativity you present will not stop them. When they are mature enough, they may transition.

Section Twelve: Your Teen's Transition

"I'm the boy that was born a girl and has to prove to myself every day that I'm man enough for the world."
— Anonymous

When younger child comes out as transgender you may realize it is easier than when they're older. This is likely true because at younger ages their lives are not as full as an older child is. For the parent, it may also be easier because they have not had their child in their life as long as a teen child. When a child tells you they are not who you knew them to be, it can come as a shock. No matter how accepting you can be hard to get past it. If you love your child without conditions, then this message may be easier to accept.

Children prefer stability. Being transgender and needing to pause puberty can be horrifying. Though they may prefer to take the blockers, it outs them because they are not developing at the same rate as other children. It takes love and awareness to facilitate your child through this time. Give them love and acceptance. Do not be your child's first bully.

There may be issues you may see are inappropriate debating with your child. This includes sexuality and sex. Your child will have to decide if they need to bank their sperm or eggs before starting hormones. The hormones leave the transgender female sterile, and the transgender male unable to conceive.

It may complicate these issues, but make sure your child receives the facts before proceeding further in their transition. Most hormone changes to the body are irreversible.

From Tanner 2 stage of puberty through their decision to begin hormones, they may take puberty blockers. The Tanner stages offer insight into where an adolescent is in their puberty. There are five stages in the Tanner index. The first Tanner stage is prior to changes from puberty. See the chart below for the expected ages in which they could start puberty. The charts show an approximation of when to discuss puberty blockers. The farther into puberty they progress, the less effect puberty blockers will have.

Puberty can be an overwhelming period for a transgender teen. Their body changes in a way they do not want it to. During this time, your child may be at their highest risk for suicide. Their transforming bodies do not fit their identity. If they cannot reveal who they are when these changes happen, their mental health can suffer.

Beyond their social transition, you may desire to discuss puberty blockers and hormones. Make these decisions ahead of time. Hormones leave many transgender people incapable of reproducing. This is both transgender males and females. If they say they want surgeries, talk with them. If you have concerns, address them.

Puberty changes in the charts below are just perceptible developments. There are further changes than these during puberty.

Tanner stages for females	Starting age	Noticeable changes
Stage 1	8th birthday	None
Stage 2	9th to 11th birthday	Breast "buds" start to form
Stage 3	Older than 12	Acne starts, armpit hair starts, fastest height increase
Stage 4	13th birthday	Period starts
Stage 5	15th birthday	Reproductive organs and genitalia fully developed

Tanner stages for males	Starting age	Noticeable changes
Stage 1	9th or 10th birthday	None
Stage 2	11th birthday	Pubic hair starts
Stage 3	13th birthday	Voice cracks, muscles grow bigger
Stage 4	14th birthday	Acne starts and armpit hair starts to grow
Stage 5	15th birthday	Facial hair starts to grow

CHAPTER FOUR: COMING OUT LATER IN LIFE

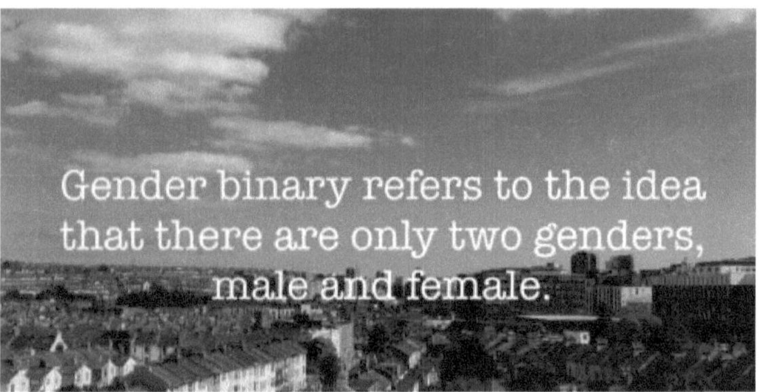

Section One: Coming Out

"All I want to know is no matter what gender I am you'll still love me like you did before."
— Anonymous

Coming out will be one of the toughest things your transgender loved one will do, whether they are coming out to you or others. Most LGBTQ people come out when they are comfortable and confident in who they are and learn to love this aspect of their identity. Your child felt confident in who they are. They also felt comfortable enough to share their identity with you. By coming out, your child is releasing the burden of coming to terms with their identity. It is essential to their future that you share their joy of self-discovery

First reactions may mirror real emotions. But those beliefs come from a place that may be uninformed. Educate yourself on what your loved one has conveyed to you. Ask questions. This provides you with a chance to understand your true feelings. Losing a child can be devastating. If they believe they cannot be true to themselves, they may leave home to embrace their new identity. Embrace them. If you have issues, try to work through them.

Show your child the same respect they showed you. Listen and do not react and allow time to absorb your feeling. This is a very emotional time for everyone. Find like-minded people to help you understand what this means. Jot down questions you may need answered. Make certain you understand and believe your child. This is a prerequisite for their eventual happiness and mental health.

By reading this book you are showing them how much you cherish and respect them. Remember this, you are not losing them, you are granting them happiness to be authentic. Be their hero.

Section Two: Coming Out to Your Children

"In trans women's eyes, I see a wisdom that can only come from having to fight for your right to be recognized as female, a raw strength that only comes from unabashedly asserting your right to be feminine in an inhospitable world."
— Julia Serano, Whipping Girl: A Transsexual Woman on Sexism and the Scapegoating of Femininity

It can be harder for someone married or in a relationship to come out. Having children increases stress and anxiety even more. Their significant others may believe they were lied to. This may be true. Most transgender people knew from an early age. The transgender person misrepresented themselves before coming out and their significant other has every right to be angry. It is still best to resolve any feelings.

Whether your children are younger or older, they may not understand why their parent is dressing and acting differently. Younger children are more accepting because they have not endured society's gender binary narrative. Losses can be extreme when children see their families split up. It is best for people affected to maintain an open mind. For cisgender spouses, their initial thoughts may be to get even. Some parents try to turn their children against the transgender parent. This can backfire. Be candid with your children and present the facts. Children are smarter than you may believe.

When a transgender parent comes out to their children, there may be various approaches to coming out to each of their children. Younger children accept the parent with little resistance. Just tell them that dad is becoming a mom, or mom is becoming a dad.

For the transgender adult to be happy, they need to transition. If the transgender parent is on hormones, the children need to understand the changes their parent will encounter.

There are stages children may pass through when their parent is transgender. Grief is one stage. This is predictable because they believe their loved one is no longer there. Help them understand their parents will always be there. They may see their parent is happier. Respect these feelings, and work through them.

The next emotion is anger. This reaction can develop throughout their parent's transition. Your children may be resentful because kids bully them at school because of their parents being transgender.

Fear. This is one emotion I think every transgender person, and those involved in their life have. For children, it can be the worry their parents will separate. This is a valid feeling. No child wants to see their parents separate, even if the reasons are legitimate. Keep every conversation open and honest. Both parents have their own worries. These will include fears for their spouses and children.

Shame is the next emotion. Though culture is more open and understanding, shame still takes place. Stereotypes aimed at transgender people may cause this shame. Shame may bring guilt to the transitioning parent.

The last emotion, relief. The relief this didn't turn out any worse. Relief may change to one of the other emotions if something negative surfaces. Remember how you handled that emotion.

To make it through unscathed, everybody must work together. They can further support those emotions or show you why they are wrong. Go to counseling. It helps to accept your feelings and discover why they may or may not be accurate.

Section Three: A Significant Other Coming Out

"We're all something we're not," he said. "Everyone of us is stuck between the person we want to be and the person we can be. And there doesn't have to be a why. All things have to do is feel right."
— Jasper Fforde, Early Riser

Coming out to a significant other may be the hardest to thing do. No matter how your spouse accepted your gender expression prior to coming out, it becomes a whole different thing when you announce you will express your identity all the time.

There is a multitude of ways to come out. Face to face may be hard and does not allow time to absorb what they have just communicated. There are those who love a person's heart and do not care what is on the outside. Couples' therapy may be essential even if you cannot preserve the relationship.

Counseling is imperative. This gives both partners a chance to work out feelings they may have wished to never face. Even the strongest of partnerships may not survive the transition. The transgender spouse should realize that their spouse is also going through a transition. Be forthright with your feelings.

Both partners need to understand other feelings. The cisgender partner needs to realize their partner wouldn't have revealed this secret unless they felt they needed to come out. The transgender partner needs to realize the cisgender partner is being confronted with something they never believed they would. The cisgender person did not sign up for being married to someone who is not who they thought they were.

Section Four: Support Your Transgender Partner

Your transgender partner will go through a lot of grief, assorted feelings, and major accomplishments. As a partner of a transgender person, you may go through many of these same feelings. It is imperative that both of you give support to each other. Many families with a transgender person in it end up breaking apart because people find it hard to accept their new loved one. This is not only the transgender person's fault for coming out. It is also the fault of the others for not trying to understand their feelings.

If you try to deny a transgender person, realize they have most likely researched this before coming out. They know they were born this way and have known most of their life who they are. Many transgender people end up with friends they see as a family. Do not let this happen. Once split apart, some families never reunite.

The transgender person's spouse/partner will also need support and understanding. This is true whether they remain with their partner or separate. Those affected will feel the impacts of the transgender person's announcement. Those closest to the transitioning person will notice it more.

The capacity for everyone affected to reach the end of this journey unharmed depends on the amount of help they receive. It will affect their mental health. Support is imperative for those affected.

There are support groups on Facebook for everyone involved. There are physical support groups in towns and cities. If you live near a city, it may be easier to locate one. Smaller towns may have support groups. Look for your local PFLAG chapter (Parents and Friends of Lesbians and Gays: later expanded to Parents, Families, and Friends of Lesbians and Gays). They help those committed to LGBTQ people's lives. You can check online for local transgender support groups. Some counselors and therapists offer support groups for a modest fee. Health insurance may also cover support groups with counselors or therapists.

Section Five: I'm Losing Them!

"I am not trapped in the wrong body; I am trapped in a world that makes very little space for bodies like mine."
— *Ivan E. Coyote, Tomboy Survival Guide*

The feeling you may lose your loved one is common. You may believe they will be a different person once they start their transition. Transgender people are only changing their outside appearance. Their personality and everything else you loved about them should remain close to the same. If they start hormones, there may be changes in their emotions. They should be happier. Because gender dysphoria is a huge factor for most you will notice they are happier. This will be visible in their love of themselves. Their mental health should improve.

The transgender person gives up the old outside for a new one. They are leaving their earlier life behind for their new congruent life. Transition is worth more than continuing life as the wrong person.

The desire to be authentic is huge. There are those who give up everything to pursue this feeling. Getting upset, calling names, and other factors will not change their minds. Once they start the transition, few go back.

Section Six: Expect the Unexpected

"Sometimes I don't know what I am. But what I would like to be on the outside --
what I want other people to see -- is a girl."
— Alyssa Brugman, Alex As Well

Throughout our lives there are a host of things that happen which are unexpected, whether good or bad. Be prepared to deal with the unexpected during this time. This can lead to anxiety or anger and can stress relationships. When a transgender person starts hormone replacement therapy (HRT), they should realize the physical changes taking place. As their partner, you need to understand these changes, too.

Try to prepare for anything unexpected. You can do so by expecting things that may happen and prepare for them. Therapists or doctors along with other things may cause delays in their transition. It helps reduce stress and anxiety. There will be tension. Try to prevent any further tension.

Disappointments will happen. There are frustrations in life. Accept them. As I worked through my transition, I had a few obstacles. I had to forego portions of my transition. It is unpleasant, but I am proud of who I am. (I am who I am)

Reactions from others can be very unexpected. Those you believe will accept may not. That one person you just know will not accept your loved one may be the most accepting and loving.

Section Seven: A Better Future Through Education and Support

"It's a tough world to find yourself in, but an even tougher one to be yourself in,"
— *Chris Colfer, Stranger Than Fanfiction*

Education and support are a necessity for a person's future. Your transgender child will be stronger if they receive good support at home. Education is essential. Try to know what your loved one is going through. Their transition will be easier.

Support in schools, jobs, and their social life will help to ensure your loved one has a smooth transition. When you do not support a transgender person, the possibility of destructive behavior and actions increase. The suicide attempt rate for transgender adults is 41 percent, and the suicide attempt rate for cisgender people is ≈ four percent. The transgender rate is 10 times higher than for cisgender people. For the whole LGBTQ community, the suicide attempt rate is ≈ 15–20 percent. Offering support for your transgender loved one can help reduce these numbers. As seen in the chart below, the differences are shocking.

There are different approaches to learn about your loved one. Books, websites and other means

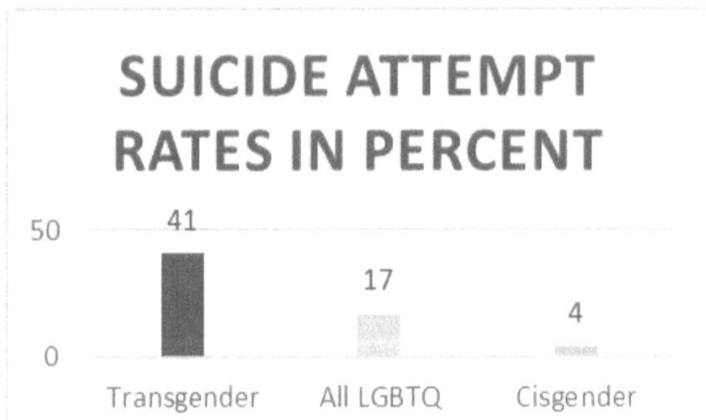

can offer you the needed information. Always check the validity of the information you use. There are people who skew data to fit their anti-transgender agenda.

Supporting transgender and LGB communities is huge. Everyone is effective, whether small or large. You can fulfill this by going to Pride, volunteering for an LGBTQ non-profit, and remaining up to date on the transgender community.

You will need to ensure their school system supports transgender students. Talk to the administration regarding their policies for transgender children. There are schools that are not affirming and may not call your child by the correct name or pronouns. This is not tolerable. Your child hopes to be safe while in school. Many transgender students drop out of school because of the harassment. Keep the avenues of conversation open between you and your child. Make certain they realize they need to report bullying. This is fundamental to their ability to make it through school. Bullies may stop once you out them.

As addressed in other parts of this book, do not become your child's first bully. This can devastate them and lead to mental health problems becoming worse. Find like-minded individuals to get help. Once you educate yourself, give back by offering support to others.

Education is a valuable asset. Knowledge is strength.

Believe in a brighter future for transgender individuals. This may be hard in our current climate but there has been a forward movement over the last decade.

Section Eight: Right and Wrong Words

*"Gender doesn't need – and doesn't have – gatekeepers. This is where the media
needs to wise up. I have no idea why news producer are asking cisgender people
for details of things they have no experience of. When it comes to trans issues, you
can either get the experience from a trans person or an opinion from a cis person.
Opinions are like assholes: everyone's got one. They're neither facts or news.*
— Juno Dawson

Words themselves do not hurt. It's the feeling and meaning of those words that can hurt or kill. Do not let anybody tell you otherwise. Transgender people are the most oppressed in the U.S. and most of the world.

There is a reference area in this book. It provides suitable and defamatory terms. It also has correct alternatives. Over time, a term's context may vary or vulgar words may become acceptable. Queer used to be derogatory. For older individuals, it still is. The younger generation grabbed queer and are proud of it.

Transvestite used to describe cross-dressers. Transgender people are not cross-dressers. When they come out and start their transition, they are committing to their identity. Transvestite is a derogatory term. Educate yourself on what are safe words and what words are not. Over time they change. Addressing a transgender individual with these terms is akin to attacking them. Though they may get surgeries, do not address them as pre-op, post-op, or non-op. You may hear a transgender person say this to another transgender individual. This does not make it okay to address transgender people this way. Why does it matter what a person has between their legs? Transgender people don't concern themselves with other people's parts. If they want to let you know, they will.

There are derogatory words formed off the term's transsexual and transgender. They use these words in the porn industry.

Remember, if it is an expression or phrase you heard many years ago, it may or may not be derogatory. LGBTQ people find it difficult to keep up with the ever-changing labels. Ask the person if they find a word offensive. People may find the word **trans** offensive. **Trans** is a reduced form of transgender.

Section Nine: Don't Out Them.

"The severity of this breach of confidence cannot be underestimated. Telling someone about your sexuality or gender identity must always be a personal decision. No person may take that decision away. Publicly outing someone robs that person of the chance to define who they are in their own terms, if they even want to. In extreme cases – as in this one – it can also put the lives of that person and their loved ones in danger."

"Outing someone ignores the many valid reasons a person may have for not choosing to be open about their sexuality to every person in their life. Concerns about personal safety to fears about discrimination at work or in their place of worship all play part in someone's decision to come out. It can be difficult, takes courage and is not necessarily a one-off event."

— Jeff Ingold, media manager at Stonewall, told indy100

It is not okay to out someone. Outing someone can be life-threatening. By outing someone they may lose friends, family, their honor, among other matters. LGBTQ people might come out more than once. It is their story, not yours. It is their one chance to prove to others who they are. Do not take this from them.

They might have a reason they have not come out to some people. Keep their secret close. They trusted you with it. Let them come out to others when they are comfortable. It may be tough keeping their secret but is it vital for their life and safety.

If your transgender loved one informs you, they did not come out to others, inquire if they are okay with you announcing it to others. If they say no, respect them. Their coming out may be unique for each person.

There are endless reasons for not coming out to everyone.

Section Ten: Updating Documents

"Identity, identification. Most in life take these two words for granted. These two words are a transgender person's whole being."
— *Stephania Kanitsch*

Your transgender loved one may elect to change their identity to reflect their new gender. This is a good chance to review life insurance policies, wills, property documents, checking accounts, and other financial and personal records. Some states seal the court record for transgender people getting a name and gender change. When sealed, they are available only through the judicial processes. It is easier to change these documents and other important papers for ease later on.

There may be many legal papers that require updating. School and college transcripts are noteworthy. Earlier jobs including time spent in the armed services are crucial.

For many transgender women, they may discover upon changing their gender their car insurance rates are lower.

Prior to changing their name and gender create a list of documents, IDs, and other paperwork which may require updates.

The older a transgender person is, the more documents there may be to change. Once you have updated everything expect something new to show up.

Section Eleven: Adult Transition

"You may say I'm a dreamer, but I'm not the only one. I hope someday you'll join us, and the world will live as one."
— John Lennon

I f they are transitioning as an adult, there may be additional decisions to make. There are approximately five steps to a full transition. Transitions have no guidelines. The first steps may be their social transition and later their medical transition (hormone replacement therapy). For others, the medical step may be the first step, so their secondary characteristics develop before coming out. During this stage, they may change their style and looks.

Different transitioning steps:

•—**Social transition,** Their social transition can start prior to them coming out to the world. Varying their gender expression at a slower pace can ease the shock for people.

There are endless ways to show your gender. They accomplish this through hair, clothes, accessories, among many other items. Let them have fun with it. It is a learning experience for everyone, including the transgender person. Everyone needs to be open about allowing them to find their identity.

•—**Medical; Hormones,** start hormones before coming out. Realize the effects of the hormones start within weeks. These effects can become noticeable within two to three months. Ensure they have a proper timeline set up for coming out that fits the effects of the hormones. It's best they are out before their breasts get bigger or their voice drops.

Therapists and endocrinologists following WPATH Standards of Care will require a one-year real-life experience. This can impede the capability of starting hormones before starting their transition. They may find it helpful using a local clinic or Planned Parenthood who accept informed consent. This allows them to start hormones sooner. There are other places that prescribe hormones with informed consent. Appointments with them may take as long or longer than the one-year real-life wait.

•—**Medical; Top surgery (transgender males),** Top surgery is the removal of the transgender males' chest and reconstructing the nipple to make the chest area more congruent to biological males. The 6,000 to 7,000-dollar cost for this surgery may be beyond some people's means. Those apt to afford this surgery find it helps their gender dysphoria.

•—**Medical; Gender confirmation surgery (GCS),** GCS may be the most affirming for the transgender person. Likewise called bottom surgery. This surgery brings their primary sex characteristics in line with their gender. GCS is beyond most transgender people's budgets. There are health insurance companies that cover the surgery. GCS can be lifesaving and affirming intervention. Most cannot afford the co-pay.

The average cost for a transgender female's GCS is $22,000. The average cost of a transgender male's surgery can go up to $100,000. Make certain you understand your co-pay ahead of time. There may be requirements to stay at a local hotel for up to a week in case problems show up. Transgender females may desire to have their breast enhancement done at the same time as their GCS.

•—**Medical; Feminine facial surgery (FFS) (transgender females)**, FFS is plastic surgery to give a more congruent face for transgender females. Few elects to have FFS because of costs and risks.

Every surgery comes with a risk. They may not prefer the effects of hormones. Educate yourselves before starting any new transition steps. Though these steps above are distinct in what they are, there are endless ways to transition. It is the transgender person's identity, and they decide on how to express that identity.

CHAPTER FIVE: COMMON INFORMATION

Section One: Societal Interference

"I'm not a societal problem. Society itself is the problem."
— Stephania Kanitsch

In a more accepting society it would be much easier to live as a transgender person. As incredible as the human body and mind are, judging others is a significant fault. There are so many stereotypes for classes, ethnicities, identities, and others. Stereotypes can weaken the ability to live. Stereotypes are untrue generalizations of classes of people. Everyone has their own views, thought processes, and belief systems.

One stereotype is transgender women are gay. When I came out to various people, their first question of me was "Are you gay?" Being transgender does not equate to being gay. A transgender individual's sexuality is as diverse as cisgender people's. Transgender people may discover their sexuality is more extensive than formerly known. When they free their minds and heart, they are more open to their feelings.

Political and religious entities start many of society's biases. Many of these biases are toxic. The present administration in Washington continues cutting services and rights for transgender people without worry about the consequences. By allowing religious liberty to exist, they are legalizing discrimination against classes of people. We will not even touch on the religious view and the transgender person except saying God is not against the transgender community. Being transgender is not a sin. To be black is not a sin. Being white is not a sin.

When their life changes because a loved one came out as transgender, their beliefs may change. I commend those who educate themselves and accept transgender people. If they oppressed transgender people in the past, they should apologize for their insincerity. I fear for the transgender individuals whose loved ones do not change and adapt. They may lose their child or other loved one. It takes education, love, and acceptance.

Section Two: Not About You

"Once you bring children into the world, it is no longer about you."
— *Tony Gaskins*

When your loved one comes out, they have learned to love and accept who they are. This is not to embarrass, make people angry or anything else. They have realized their authenticity. Few people achieve this in their lifetime.

Do not require them to accommodate you by communicating your preference that they do not express their gender outside your doors. This is their identity, you are asking them to not be authentic.

Do not let your acceptance come with caveats. This projects to them you do not respect their identity. If you are embarrassed, that is your feeling. They cannot make you embarrassed. This can be detrimental and create mental health problems. Transgender people take their lives because they relate this to not being able to live their authentic life.

To take a person's identity away is denying their existence. Other negative treatment can make them feel like a second-class citizen. This is unacceptable. They should treat no one this way.

Section Three: Education is Essential

---

*"Gender needs to be taught about in schools, the earlier the better. My death
needs to mean something. My death needs to be counted in the number of
transgender people who commit suicide this year. I want someone to look at that
number and say 'that's f***ed up' and fix it. Fix society. Please."*
— Leelah Alcorn

Knowledge is power. We gain knowledge through educating yourself and from real-life experiences. Your loved one made a huge choice. How far they go in their transition can influence the knowledge they require.

Education is essential to survive in this world. Most people do not understand what being transgender involves. Many people remark they have never met a transgender person. They may see them in a restroom without realizing it. It is not surgeries and hormones. It is legitimacy and communicating that legitimacy. Even if they only go through their social transition, there is still a lot to learn. As a loved one, try to stay up to date.

There are many words for the different genders under the transgender spectrum, how to transition, positive and demeaning words, words unique to transgender populations, along with other subjects.

There is an appendix with terms unique to the transgender community. It is comprehensive, but there are more words beyond what this book presents. This book supplies many of the familiar words used in the book.

Section Four: Are They Non-binary?

"I'll be okay even if I don't understand how I don't want to be a girl, but also don't want to be a man,"
—*Courtney Carola, Have Some Pride: A Collection Of LGBTQ+ Inspired Poetry*

Transgender is an umbrella term for anybody whose gender is not the same as their birth sex. Non-binary is also under that umbrella. Some transgender people may not classify themselves as any gender. They prefer non-binary only (enbees). They may express their uncertainty with more fluid gender expression. This is commonplace.

A gender fluid person is an individual who may vary their expression. Be open to what they are trying to figure out, this is their journey. It is essential they discover themselves.

Non-binary is everything outside the gender binary. For transgender males and females, they may identify within the binary (male/female). A greater segment of young individuals is coming out as non-binary.

We consider Genderqueer to be non-binary, but many individuals consider genderqueer offensive.

Non-binary people may identify themselves as two or more genders ("bigender, trigender or pangender"). They may label themselves as having no gender.

Non-binary people may prefer to use gender-neutral pronouns such as they, them, and theirs. Others are ze, sie, hir, co, and ey.

There are some states and countries that have passed statutes allowing individuals to choose a neutral gender for identification. This is a forward movement.

In a recent transgender survey one-third of those responding selected non-binary.

Section Five: What's Next?

"I never realized how intimidating it could be to be authentic,"
— Jordon Johnson, Love, Always: Partners of Trans People on Intimacy, Challenge
& Resilience

After transitioning and achieving congruence, what is next for your transgender loved one. Enjoy life as the new person they are. Be happy with who they are and proud of their accomplishments.

Give back to the transgender community. It is never the wrong thing to do. Even if they are stealth (pass as the gender they are expressing) they can give back. Your loved one and you can serve for a local transgender or LGBTQ resource center, or other related local non-profits. Manning phone banks for non-profits who advocate helps the whole LGBTQ community. Sign up with national advocacy groups and volunteer for events that affect local and national issues or events. There are many more ways than listed.

If your city or town has an LGBTQ Chamber of Commerce, you can locate both local and national entities that may love your support. Giving back is gratifying and a valuable asset.

The transgender population is 1.4 million individuals. The need for allies is more significant with the present administration and the ripping apart of transgender rights. Federal and state governments continue signing into a law hurtful and restricting measures.

When they legislate discrimination, it abuses the oppressed. This makes it unsafe to be transgender and out.

Section Six: No More Deadnames

*"So y'all my folks won't call me Ellie cause they're 'not ready.' How do I explain to
them for like the fortieth time that deadnaming me makes me feel like an 'it'
rather than someone who is developing a true self?"*
— Ellie

Deadnames are the names parents gave transgender people at birth once they have changed their name. The deadname may seem to be a harsh phrase, but the person fitting the old name is no longer here. I use it in this book because we use it throughout the transgender community. It is a deadname once a transgender person decides their new name fitting their gender. It can hard for loved ones to accept this. Surviving in a body that doesn't fit your name is stressful.

Transgender people understand the accidental use of their deadnames. This is true when the loved one has known the transgender person for a while. When a person uses a transgender person's deadname with evil intent, they may consider it bullying.

It can take time to remember their new name. They may correct you often. This is to help you in remembering their names. They will also correct the pronouns you use. This is commonplace and not meant to be mean.

Do not reveal their deadname to others who do not know who they are. They are no longer that person. You may out them if they are stealth. Only the transgender person should inform others of their deadname.

If others use their deadname, correct them. The more you correct others, the easier it may be to help them understand why it is so important. Educate others on why it is harmful to continue using their deadnames.

Section Seven: Affirmation, Love, and Support

"Make sure you have friends (and family) lined up who can give you love, support,
and affirmation and support for the holidays."
— Anonymous

When we do not give transgender people love, support, and affirmation, it has very definite effects on their mental health and lives of their present and future. Suicide attempts for those supported and affirmed drop to the same level as cisgender people.

If you have an issue with your transgender loved one's new gender identity and transition, do not condemn them. It shows your loved one you do not love them enough to accept their identity.

If they are under 18, they may believe they can never be themselves. Their gender dysphoria can become worse. They may consider running away to be themselves. Forty percent of juveniles on the streets are LGBTQ children. A stunning 67 percent of transgender teens end up in the sex trades. If they volunteered themselves, they may end up controlled by sex-traffickers. There are parents who disavow their transgender children. Later they may discover they were mistaken and attempt to rectify the relationship. Your child may not want to rectify the relationship if it has hurt them.

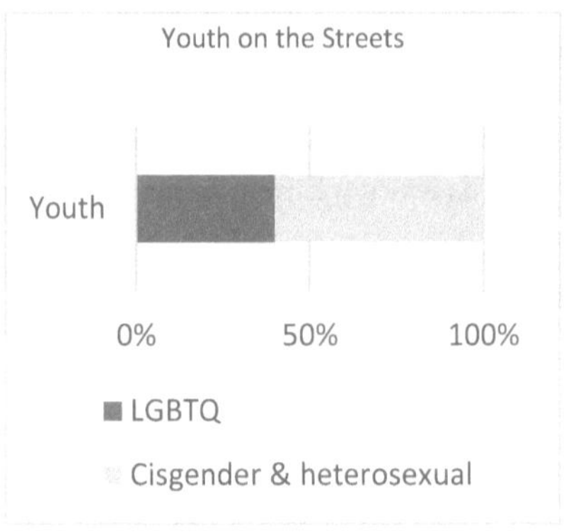

Section Eight: Affirmation

"we know it is really important for parents to support their kids in their trans identities Kuvalanka said.
— Kate Kuvalanka

The transgender person needs to realize it can take time for loved ones to come to terms with their announcement. This announcement can be difficult for anyone to accept. The reality is it can turn everyone's world upside-down, but it is essential to try not to show negativity. Educate yourself on what being transgender is.

Try not to be impatient. Become comfortable with the idea your loved one is transgender. Most transgender people knew from a young age there was a difference. Your child had time to educate themselves on the complexities of what being transgender entails however, this is new for you.

They should know what transitioning is when they come out to you. They may want to do everything at first. As time moves on, they may elect not to carry out certain parts of their transition. If their gender dysphoria doesn't get worse and the gender dysphoria isn't regarding their genitalia, they may find happiness with just taking hormones. Your child may discover the peace of mind they seek in achieving a minimum transition. As far as gender dysphoria, it may diminish but never dissipate.

Section Nine: Listen, Understand

"When I say empathic listening, I mean listening with the intent to understand. I mean seeking first to understand, to really understand. It's an entirely different paradigm. Empathic (from empathy) listening gets inside another person's frame of reference. You look out through it, you see the world the way they see the world, you understand their paradigm, you understand how they feel."
— Stephen R. Covey, The 7 Habits of Highly Effective People

L istening to their wishes is important. Keep the paths of conversation open. This is vital for both the parents and transgender loved ones to come out the other end unscathed.

For many, reading a person's body language can be easy. Make certain your body language matches what you say.

If a subject requires you to educate yourself, use a reputable website. There are groups who twist the research done on transgender people to fit their agenda. There is an appendix in this book that provides contact information for many of the reputable organizations that may have the information you need.

I try to remain current with ongoing research. Searching by unique subjects will present studies, surveys and research being accomplished.

Stay away from religious or political sites. They may alter their data to satisfy agendas they may have. Contact me at info@SpanningGenderBooks.com and I will attempt to offer information you have requested.

Section Ten: Positive Support

"Having courage does not mean we are unafraid. Having courage and showing courage mean we face our fears. We are able to say, 'We have fallen and will get up.'"
— *Maya Angelou*

Throughout this book we have talked about support, love, and affirmation. If they request something you deem as unsafe for their transition, it is okay to say no. You should, however, offer some kind of explanation of why you do not want them to proceed with it. Ensure both sides have a productive and positive interaction. Provide them with references you use to defend your position. Give them a chance to challenge you and time to complete their own research. Prepare for the chance they have already explored the subject and have a different answer. If your feelings remain the same, make certain you can support your reasoning. Do not vacillate back and forth.

Stay firm in your conviction and choices. Only waiver when your loved one is proposing an uninformed or risky act. It is crucial to offer a transparent canvas to portray their life. It is their life. Only intervene when needed.

Do not allow your emotions to get the best of you. This is a moment for you to show love and support. If you are emotional, you may express feelings you do not mean. You cannot take back anything once it's said. They may have gender dysphoria and anxiety. This can affect their mental health.

If you are emotional over a topic, give yourself time before reacting.

Section Eleven: Discrimination

"Straight Americans need an education of the heart and soul. They must understand – to begin with - how it can feel to spend years denying your own deepest truths, to sit silently through classes, meals, and church services while people you love toss off remarks that brutalize your soul."
— Bruce Bawer

Discrimination runs rampant in the transgender community. If you face discrimination or stereotypes, try to have facts to disavow their claims. There are stereotypes targeted toward transgender individuals. Stereotypes and myths concerning transgender people are easy to prove wrong.

Religious and political organizations may start some of these stereotypes. Bathroom bills do not give security when someone wishes to harm others. No transgender man or woman has ever assaulted a person in a restroom. Transgender people use restrooms for the same purposes everyone else does.

By fighting discrimination, you are providing a better future for transgender people. Transgender people are where gay people were 50 years ago. State and federal governments have quashed many of the transgender community's rights in the last three years. Speaking to your representatives and senators in Congress helps offer a better future. Volunteer for groups offering advocacy for transgender people. Vote for lawmakers advocating for transgender people. Most individual's political views are unalterable, but to help transform culture, people must open their hearts.

Contribute to local and national transgender and LGB groups who provide advocacy and support. There are many organizations that advocate for the transgender community. They push to end the backward movement. They need all the help they can get.

Whether stereotypes target a specific individual or a whole class of individuals, it can create anxiety. There is an ongoing movement to erase transgender people from society by denying their ability to exist. Bathroom bills, religious liberty acts, redefining what gender is, and restricting transgender individuals from the armed services are forms of discrimination.

Consider pictures, composed and communicated comments, non-verbal signals discriminatory. Bigotry is discrimination.

Types of discrimination:

People do not always realize they are discriminating against someone. However, there are those who do it with harmful intent. It is a means of denying a person's worth, self-esteem and deny their existence.

There are a lot of marginalized groups that society discriminates against. Discrimination, hate, and fear start when a person or group varies from society's norms. It may be religious. They may assume only their religion is right. They then discriminate against those who are not the same religion. It can be sex, gender, disabilities, affectional orientation, ethnicity, color, country of origin, gender identity and others.

There are five different discrimination types.

Direct Discrimination

Direct discrimination is the easiest to see. Direct discrimination is when they treat a person or group with cruel intent. They perpetuate this by specific real and perceived characteristics. Their association with a marginalized person may be a rationale for discrimination.

Example: A cake shop will not create a cake because the client transgender or a bar owner declines to serve them because they are transgender.

Direct discrimination is a malicious form of discrimination. This is because the offender aims it at the group being discriminated against.

Indirect Discrimination

Statutes and regulations implemented in haste which they write so they effect specific groups or classes. This discrimination is harder to prove. They may pass guidelines, practices or laws stating health or safety concerns. They justify bathroom laws by claiming safety considerations for cisgender females because transgender women use women's restrooms.

Associative Discrimination

Associative discrimination is when they discriminate against an individual because of their association with an oppressed class. An illustration is to stroll into a church or restaurant, and they reject you because of your loved one's identity. Associative discrimination gives the loved one a look at the hate discrimination yields.

Perceptive Discrimination

Perceptive discrimination is when an individual discriminates against another person or group because of perceived protected characteristics. Perceptive discrimination is when a person thinks someone is disabled. They may not be but are being discriminated against.

Harassment

Harassment is when someone attacks an individual with protected characteristics through spoken terms, expressions, composed expressions, pictures, and jokes. Harassment and bullying go hand in hand. When a person harasses someone they do it through various means of intolerance.

Subtle Discrimination

Subtle discrimination is when an individual pulls back or treats an individual different because the individual has specific characteristics. They may not realize they are doing it or look at it as discrimination. An illustration is going into a business and individuals move away from you. They may believe if they are too close to a transgender person they will become transgender. Don't laugh. People believe this.

More on Discrimination

- — Two-thirds suffering a hate crime or event did not disclose it.
- — Fewer than one in 10 victims who reported hate crimes and events to the police had it lead to a conviction.
- — Thirty-eight percent of transgender individuals have encountered physical intimidation. Eighty-one percent have experienced silent harassment. (e.g. being glared at/whispering). [5]
- — If harassment and discrimination continue for any period, the victim can experience worsening depression and physical health effects.

The Cycle of Oppression

Oppression is when a stronger person exploits a person or group to cast them as less than human. It presents as a continuous cycle of unjust treatment of exploited classes. Oppression comes in many, if not unlimited forms. Government rescinding protections for LGBTQ people and bathroom bills. You may find it interesting in how this puts transgender individuals in a less than human light by denying their existence.

This material provides you knowledge of what oppression is, how it starts, and how it can affect transgender individuals. This can give insight into how to stop oppression.

First Step of Oppression: Differences

Society's current culture expects everyone to live within an unwritten set of social practices or norms. These practices can refer to any class or group. (Cis-normative: the theory there is only two genders). Society puts everyone in the gender binary when filling out forms, they have only male or female checkboxes. There are just male or female restrooms. Male or female clothes. There are many more examples.

People see you in a different light when you refuse to live by these social practices or norms. The stereotype transgender women are men in dresses still exists. By educating people, the effect of current stereotypes continuing to perpetuate lessens. Education does not fix everything, but it is an excellent place to start.

Second Step of Oppression: Stereotypes

When they continue to retell the differences between a group or person, they become stereotypes. Society then applies these stereotypes to everyone in that class. This even happens with white heterosexual cisgender males. They are not in a protected class, but because many in politics fit this definition, they put them in this group with the stereotypes aboutt them. A stereotype is a preconceived or oversimplified generalization about a group or class of people. Stereotypes can be both positive and negative. People face these stereotypes from their family, friends, and society. The only problem with stereotypes, positive or negative is they are inaccurate. No two individuals are the same.

One of the more hurtful stereotypes is transgender individuals have confusion regarding who they are and have mental health problems.

Transgender individuals access mental health at greater percentages which can be from the harassment they face.

Stereotypes grasp oppressed groups and keep the cycle of oppression turning. Society needs to accept that everyone is unique.

Third Step of Oppression: Prejudice

They define prejudices as generalizations aimed at classes or identities. They are negative or limiting assumptions. One prejudice is people with HIV+ are gay. This prejudice started as HIV appeared first with gay men at more frequent occurrences. This stereotype was and still is false. HIV+ is also a prejudice against transgender individuals.

When a transgender woman desires to donate blood, the form they fill out asks the same questions as gay males. Some assume transgender women are gay and prefer sex with gay and straight males. This is wrong in many respects.

Fourth Step of Oppression: Discrimination

When they direct these biases at a targeted class to produce misery it becomes discrimination. If they have prejudice and power, they use the power to withhold access or hinder someone's capability of gaining resources. They may do this through regulation, exclusion of service, or not supplying equal rights to the targeted group. Discrimination affects people, unique for each one.

Education is so essential to ending this hate directed at already marginalized groups.

Fifth Step of Oppression: Oppression

Oppression is hatred on a societal level. Oppression applies to whole classes of people. It starts at a much grander scale. A class with power can oppress a weaker class. States lacking nondiscrimination laws for transgender individuals are oppressing them. They are granting individuals and institutions the right to discriminate.

Oppressed communities become victims of violence and further discrimination. For other ethnicities, oppression can end up multiplying. This makes it harder to exist in society. Transgender women of color are a target more so than white transgender females. Changing society is imperative. If reform does not take place, the transgender community will face more hatred and violence.

Sixth Step of Oppression: Internalized Oppression

Targeted classes of people hear these misrepresentations over time and start accepting them as facts. They may hear these stereotypes from an early age. It is easy to understand how internalized oppression can influence those already oppressed.

When they encounter these stereotypes from an early age, they remain with a person into adulthood. Younger transgender individuals may not have experienced the hate and oppression of older transgender people. This may be why they see it is easier to come out.

Seventh Step of Oppression: Stereotypes Accepted as Real

When a person or a class accepts the stereotypes and oppression, they may not desire to accomplish something because they have heard over and over their class of people cannot do it. This can restrict the ability of a person to exist in society if they believe they cannot compete with others because of their identity.

This depresses and oppresses. We need to stop this cycle and allow everyone to flourish.

The Cycle Repeats

You can see how this cycle progresses. The diagram below shows how this cycle runs, and how each step feeds into the next. People use oppression to manipulate groups of individuals.

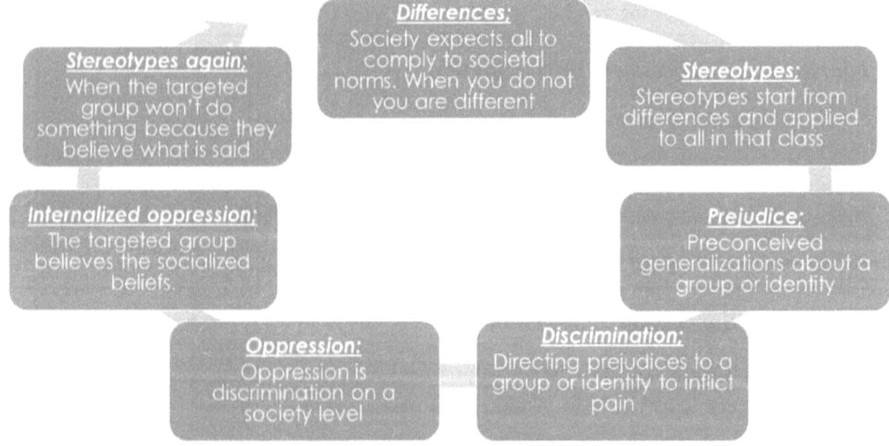

CHAPTER SIX: BE AN ALLY

Section One: Ask Questions

"Do not follow where the path may lead. Go, instead, where there is no path and leave a trail."
— Ralph Waldo Emerson

There are no stupid questions. If you need to know what your transgender loved one is doing, question them. if they desire to start a new step in their transition, ask questions. Make sure they are ready. Always stay on a topic with whatever you are discussing or questioning. Do not backtrack to previous topics. There may seem to be an endless supply of questions. This will apply even if they only go through their social transition. Discussing an old topic may appear as not being a settled topic. If it does not settle the topic, explain why you are bringing it back up.

If you have issues with them going through surgeries, be sincere. When you are not sincere, you can slip up and reveal to them your disapproval.

When discussing HRT, make clear you understand the topic and issues. Changes from hormones are permanent. If they are a child or young adult, inquire if they want to have children. Once they start hormones, transgender women will become infertile. Transgender men may discover they cannot conceive. A transgender female's voice and facial hair may lighten but will not diminish. Transgender male's breasts may become smaller but will never go back to where they were.

The appendix has a chart providing the more prominent effects of hormones.

Think before you talk. What you may believe is a compliment may not be. Know what you are getting ready to say before responding.

When they go through their transition, it becomes a commitment to who they are. When they are sure of who they are, the majority never de-transition.

Section Two: Statistics

"Suicide," Annie adds. "They kill themselves; you know. And I want a happy daughter, not a dead son."
— Mother of an eight-year-old child with gender issues.

S tatistics on the transgender community are outrageous. Allies offer help and support to decrease some of these statistics. It is so vital for you to become your loved one's advocate. The transgender community's population is so little they cannot fight this fight by themselves. They depend on their allies, other LGBTQ people, and loved ones to support them in their quest for equal rights.

With 41 percent of transgender individuals attempting suicide, it becomes obvious something needs to change. Of those 41 percent, 90 percent attempted suicide before 25 years of age.

This is only one of the many factors which make the transgender community vulnerable. While the suicide attempt rate may be outrageous, many other factors exist that are unbelievable. It is your loved one who now finds they are in an oppressed group of people. Support, love, and understanding go far in helping.

Statistics on transgender people:

• — Transgender people sign up for the military in greater percentages than cisgender people. Of the 1.4 million transgender individuals in the U.S., 15,600 were serving in the military prior to the current ban on transgender people. [6]

• — Of those who have transitioned, 78 percent of post-transition transgender people find pleasure in their lives. [7]

• — Gender confirmation surgery (GCS) was first carried out in the U.S. at Johns Hopkins University in 1966. Lili Elbe, a German national, received the first-ever recorded GCS surgery in 1930. There were others before her but they didn't receive recognition The movie The Danish Girl is a biography of Lili's life. [8]

• — Transgender people are nothing new. Transgender people have existed since human kinds beginning. The documented account of transgender people dates to the Assyrian society in the 25th century B.C. [9]

• — There are parts of society that believe transgender people are a risk to others when using the bathroom corresponding to their gender. Transgender people are the ones at a higher risk of violence using the restroom of their sex at birth. [10]

• — Transgender people are not gay. Their orientation varies as much as cisgender people. [11]

• — A larger percentage of transgender people live below the poverty level than cisgender people. A study identified that a transgender person was four times more prone to generate less than $10,000 yearly. [12]

• — Twenty-three percent of transgender individuals have dealt with discrimination when looking for a residence. This research shows that ten percent of transgender people interviewed have faced eviction because of their gender identity. [13]

• — Healthcare for transgender people is deficient in many areas. Many do not have health coverage. Their healthcare providers may discriminate against them. It is conceivable they may not get care for things restricted to people of distinct genders (prostate check, mammogram, and others). There is a 50 percent chance of transgender people getting HIV (for transgender females). [14]

• — DSM-IV (the prior DSM) designated gender identity disorder (GID) as a mental health diagnosis. People continue to believe this. DSM-V replaced GID with gender dysphoria. This accomplished nothing in appeasing the critics. People assume transgender people are confused because of their identity. In society, it is tough to maintain a tranquil life if they look at you as strange. This can contribute to more stress, which can contribute to greater mental health complications. Greater mental health complications lead to more physical health problems.

• — A large proportion of transgender women of color lose their lives every year by homicide. They are losing their lives for being their authentic selves. Murders of transgender individuals are at an epidemic level. This does not make the news. Year after year the number of homicides climbs even higher.

• — Older transgender people who are now coming out knew from an early age how to hide their identity and either "man up" or "woman up". This protected them in a society that did not acknowledge who they were. They have pressed forward since then. There are many negative or uncertain feelings surrounding transgender individuals even still.

• — In the United States, 0.6 percent of the adult populace (1.4 million people) identify as transgender. [15]

• — Transgender children and youth experience elevated levels of tormenting and violence at school. [16]

• — Anti-LGBTQ violence affects transgender people at higher levels.

• — Transgender people suffer higher amounts of police violence. [17]

• — An article determined that transgender people are 3.7 times more prone to encounter police violence than cisgender survivors and victims of anti-LGBTQ violence (LGBQ). [17]

• — The risk is higher for transgender females. They are four times more likely to have endured police violence. [17]

• — Transgender people experience higher percentages of harassment and discrimination in the workplace.

• — Transgender people experience higher-than-average amounts of housing discrimination and homelessness. [18]

• — Transgender people find themselves homeless at a figure of twice the nationwide average. [18]

• — They are less than half as likely to own their own home vs. the average American. [18]

• — Nineteen percent of transgender people say someone has refused them housing. [19]

• — They have evicted eleven percent of transgender people, leaving them more exposed to attacks and less apt to report those attacks. [18]

Transgender youth

• — Gender-expansive youth experience a 78 percent chance of negative connotations toward LGBTQ people before coming out. [19]

• — Transgender youth are over two times as likely to run into ridicule or mockery by family members for their identity than cisgender LGBQ youth. [19]

• — Fifty-one percent of transgender youth never use the restroom or locker room matching their gender identity. This may be because school districts are not supporting them. [20]

• — Thirty-one percent express their gender in some form displaying their gender identity in school. [20]

• — Other students address transgender students one in three times by their correct name. [20]

• — Other students address transgender students one in five times by their correct pronouns. [20]

• — Less than a quarter of transgender youth believe they can be themselves at home. [20]

• — Seventy-seven percent of transgender youth have faced unwanted sexual remarks, jokes, and gestures. [20]

• — Only 16 percent of transgender youth always feel protected at school. [21]

• — Fifty percent of transgender youth have suffered personal threats because of their identity. [22]

• — Only 36 percent of transgender youth's parents become engaged with the larger LGBTQ community. [19]

• — Ninety-five percent of transgender youth have trouble sleeping at night. [23]

• — Eighty-five percent of transgender youth and 82 percent of LGBQ youth rate their stress on a scale of one to ten at five. [23]

• — A rough estimate of 41 percent of LGBTQ youth received emotional counseling in the last year. [19]

• — Only 26 percent of LGBTQ youth feel safe in the classroom. [19]

• — Seventy-three percent of LGBTQ youth have experienced verbal threats because of their actual or perceived LGBTQ identity. [19]

Section Three: Educate Others

"You educate a man; you educate a man. You educate a woman; you educate a generation."
—Brigham Young

Education is crucial. I mention this throughout this book because it is so important for the transgender communities future. There are individuals who do not understand or their beliefs outweigh the facts. These individuals will not change. Educated allies can enlighten others. Those I talk to are astonished and grateful for informing them.

The fear people display is their weakness and fear of the unknown. The sole reference they may have to what transgender is may only be through the stereotypes they have heard. It is imperative to correct those who say something negative to your transgender loved one. They may not wish to understand the facts. Do not waste time with them, just hope there comes a time those with closed minds open them to everyone.

There are many sites providing references, printable PDF documents, and other sources for material. The best providers are advocacy groups. There is one for LGBTQ children in school. They are the Gay, Lesbian & Straight Education Network organization (GLSEN). If you do not find what you are searching for contact me through my website https://SpanningGenderBooks.com or send me an email at info@SpanningGenderBooks.com. I will make every attempt to answer your questions as quick as possible.

Section Four: Staying Safe

"This world would be a whole lot better if we just made an effort to be less horrible to one another."
— Ellen Page

Transgender people may find their ability to exist in society hard. There are steps a transgender person can take to make their journeys in public a little safer. Remember there is strength in numbers.

There is no sure way of ensuring the safety of your loved one. There are ways you can help them survive and not put themselves in a harmful situation. This is important information. Global deaths of transgender people take place at a pace of over one per day. Most are transgender women of color.

Transgender women experience a 72 percent of LGBTQ hate crimes.

Stay Safe:

• — Locate or establish a transgender group of individuals. Staying in groups offers a better focus on a person's identity. Numbers offer security.

• — Never Go Out by Yourself. This is part of building communities. If you go out or wander into a strange business or bar, make certain to have a partner with you. Going out by yourself is risky for everybody but more so for transgender people. They target transgender people at a higher rate than cisgender people.

Where legal, carry mace, pepper spray, stun guns, etc. I do not encourage using a handgun to protect yourself. The above products allow you extra time to leave the scene.

• — Select a safe place to live. Some regions are safer than others for transgender individuals. Urban spaces are safer. Rural spaces are not as safe. I live in a small town outside Austin. I have faced some hate. There are states which are safer than others. Do your research. If you have the means move to a safer location.

• — When entering a new business, locate the exits. You never know if you may need them.

• — Know who your neighbors are. This helps in knowing who they are. Your neighbor may be an ally you did not know you had.

• — Create a safety list. Your list can include scenarios in case you walk into a violent situation. Experiencing a violent assault is not the moment to figure out what to do.

Going Out:

• — Take a partner when you go out. As explained above, it is essential to have another person with you, particularly when going somewhere you haven't been to before. If there is a risk of violence, keep them close.

• — Stay alert. Keep cognizant of what's going on. If you do not have a close friend to go with, make certain you remain aware of your surroundings.

• — Trust your gut. If things appear dangerous, regard them as dangerous. Make sure you separate yourself from the incident.

• — Watch your drink. Never leave your drink unattended. Do not accept a drink from anybody. You never know what they may have put in it. If you leave it for a few seconds, have the bartender pour you a fresh drink.

• — Make sure someone you trust knows your plans. If those plans vary, update your friend, including if you hook up with someone.

• — If you use controlled substances, including liquor, realize your limits. Even if you are having a good time, stop at your limit and drink something non-alcoholic.

• — If you are out with others, use a safety word and use it if you notice something amiss.

• — If you contact someone online, make certain you give the individual's name, handle and other relevant info to your friends. Meet only in well-traveled areas.

• — If a situation appears unsafe, say no. Try to let any new hookups know you are transgender. There are some transgender individuals who say it is no one's business. Assess the situation. If your relationship advances beyond one date, explain ahead of time.

• — Do your homework. Know ahead of time the layout of establishments you enter, the crowd it brings in, and every exit beforehand.

Always stay aware of your surroundings. Plan your exit if trouble develops. Do not consider going near transphobic businesses.

Until this world understands hate, hurt, and judgment can harm a person's psyche, the transgender community must remain vigilant. You are your own safety system. Have someone with you when possible. When viable, make use of every sense you have to give you the safest atmosphere achievable.

One last note. If you get into a situation, recognize it is not your fault. Stay safe and call authorities when able. Do not let someone else's hate keep you from happiness!

Section Five: Validating Your Loved One

"An amazing thing happens when you stop seeking approval and validation: You find it. People are naturally drawn like magnets to those who know who they are and cannot be shaken!"
— Mandy Hale, The Single Woman: Life, Love, and a Dash of Sass

The single most important item to remember is validating your loved one's new identity. Accomplish this by embracing them and cherishing who they are. Even if your initial response wasn't the best, you can still show them your love by embracing and validating them.

Younger kids can sense when you do not acknowledge who they are. Most people learn body language at a young age.

This is essential to offer them a brighter future.

Ways your responses may not validate your transgender loved one:

• — Do not misgender them. Use the correct pronouns. It may be tough using their pronouns and a new name, but over time it becomes easier.

By not addressing them correctly, you deny their true identity. This is a tough journey for everyone. Show respect. Make sure they show respect.

• — Do not make excuses for using their deadname, even by accident. Transgender people understand this will happen. Apologize when a mistake happens. This experience is a large learning curve for everyone. It can take time to learn and use the correct pronouns and names. You may apologize often. This takes place with transgender people when they are interacting with other transgender individuals. It becomes harder when the longer people know the person who has come out.

• — Do not say you understand something if you don't. Most people do not understand what being transgender is. When you pursue to find out, you show you care and are validating them.

You are using this book to educate yourself. This shows them you care for their future. Use this knowledge to teach others.

When an individual doesn't embrace the identity of the transgender person, it can burden the relationship and make them feel unloved.

• — Respect their boundaries. You may assume it is within your right to give a birthday card that addresses their former identity. Many transgender people hate to have reminders of their former identities, including pictures. Try to stick to their choices. By having pictures of their previous identity out or putting them online you may set off their gender dysphoria. Inquire if they are okay with you doing this. If they are not, try not to.

Do your best not to confront them on the boundaries they have set.

It can be hard letting go of your old memories of them. This is understandable. Now is the best time to start.

It is okay to struggle with their disclosure. They are becoming someone different.

• — Do not negotiate. Even though you may assume you are protecting them by negotiation, this may not be how it looks to them.

If you set boundaries, it can show you are not okay with this.

• — Do not neglect their emotions. You may grieve. This may be because you sense you are giving up your loved one. This is brief. Your loved one's adverse and hurt feelings can last a lifetime. Do not harm the rapport you have with them. Everyone wants the other individual to understand their pain. This may not be the ideal moment.

This is a situation where you may require outside aid. Find a therapist. One who specializes as a gender therapist can be the best for not just your loved one, but you.

Section Six: Stand Up to Hate

"It is better to be hated for what one is than to be loved for what one isn't."
— *Andre Gider / Writer*

The transgender community experiences a disproportionate amount of hate and violence. It reveals itself in separate ways. LGBTQ people also direct hate toward transgender individuals. There is even hate and transphobia within the transgender community.

There are factions within the transgender community who encounter more hate and violence than others. Transgender women of color experience an extreme amount of violence. Transgender women encounter more than transgender men. There are more stereotypes involving transgender women than transgender men.

Transphobia used to be much worse but still occurs. Transphobia can cause fear, hate, disbelief or mistrust of people. They use transphobia against transgender people, those considered being transgender, or whose gender expression does not agree with the gender binary. Fear in society starts when people see others as different. Fear of the unknown may harvest transphobia in people. If they claim religious liberty, this claim is still transphobic and bigoted.

Transgender people do not differ from anyone else. They live, love, and work like everyone else. They are not sex freaks, stained or unreliable.

Transphobia shows itself in distinct forms. These forms include negative points of view and convictions, irrational fear and misunderstanding, abuse up to and including assault, harassing, name-calling, defamatory remarks, using incorrect name and pronouns, and hostility to and prejudice against transgender people.

Transphobia can be subtle or obvious forms of discrimination.

They may pass them over for a job, housing or healthcare. Their healthcare may be minimal because the healthcare professional does not wish to serve them.

Negative effects from transphobia:

- *Suicide*
- *Fear*
- *Isolation*
- *Depression*
- *Hopelessness*
- *Anxiety*

If they face transphobia, there are places to seek support. This is fundamental if they have depression or suicidal intentions. This is a brief list of places to locate support if they experience hate:

- — National organizations. The appendix includes a broader list.
- — Online Facebook or other social media groups.
- —Local Support groups.
- —Older transgender individuals. They may have coping techniques that aid to free your concerns. Words of wisdom are priceless.
- — Contact the Trevor Project if they have thoughts or are planning suicide. They have an anonymous chatline and phone bank. Their phone number is: **1-866-488-7386**

Their site is:

https://www.thetrevorproject.org/

- — Another group to call is Trans Lifeline. They can help them through their dilemma. They staff Trans Lifeline with transgender people. It is specific to transgender people. They are the best resource if they associate the crisis with their identity status. Their phone numbers are: US: **877-565-8860 Canada: 877-330-6366**

Students may ask for help from their teachers, counselors or school administrators. It is unfortunate some school systems are not supportive of transgender students. It is essential your transgender loved one report harassment and bullying to school officials and you.

Recognizing hateful acts is not always easy. An individual should figure out what is hateful and hurtful. This publication furnishes many examples of what is hateful and hurtful. Below is a list to support you in your understanding of what may be detrimental.

Forms of hate against transgender individuals:

- — Outing someone as being transgender.
- — Do not believe stereotypes. Work to resolve them.
- — Never allow yourself or others to inquire about their genitalia. This is no one's business.
- — Do not inquire what their affectional orientation is.
- — Comments may appear legitimate, but can be hurtful.
- — Show them you are an ally.

• — Do not use slurs or demeaning terms or phrases. Many people may not understand they have said something demeaning.

• — If they do not know a transgender person's name or preferred pronouns, have them ask.

• — A transgender person is not only transgender. They are humans. Their lives do not focus on their identity.

BIBLIOGRAPHY

[1]   "The Trevor Project, Facts About Suicide," [Online]. Available: https://www.thetrevorproject.org/resources/preventing-suicide/facts-about-suicide/.

[2]   J. Seaton, "The Washington Post, Homeless rates for LGBT teens are alarming, but parents can make a difference," 29 March 2017. [Online]. Available: https://www.washingtonpost.com/news/parenting/wp/2017/03/29/homeless-rates-for-lgbt-teens-are-alarming-heres-how-parents-can-change-that/?noredirect=on&utm_term=.b9de6879ea2b. [Accessed 2019].

[3]   WPATH, "https://www.wpath.org/publications/soc," [Online]. Available: https://www.wpath.org/publications/soc.

[4]   "Transgender Trend," [Online]. Available: https://www.transgendertrend.com/puberty-blockers/.

[5]   "Retrieved from LGBT Facts and Figures:," [Online]. Available: http://www.stonewall.org/media/lgbt-facts-and figures.

[6]   "National Center for Transgender Equality," National Center for Transgender Equality, Issues/Military Veterans, [Online]. Available: https://transequality.org/issues/military-veterans.

[7]   "Counseling transgender persons and their families By Al Carlozzi August 1, 2017," Counseling Today, 1 August 2017. [Online]. Available: https://ct.counseling.org/2017/08/counseling-transgender-persons-families/.

[8]   "Sex reassignment surgery (male-to-female)," [Online]. Available: https://en.wikipedia.org/wiki/Sex_reassignment_surgery_(male-to-female).

[9]   "Transgender History," Wikipedia, [Online]. Available: https://en.wikipedia.org/wiki/Transgender_history.

[10]   J. Brady, "When a Transgender Person Uses a Public Bathroom Who is at Risk," 15 May 2016. [Online]. Available: https://www.npr.org/2016/05/15/477954537/when-a-transgender-person-uses-a-public-bathroom-who-is-at-risk NPR, Jeff Brady, May 15, 2016, 7:48 AM ET.

[11]   G. Lopez, "Transgender people: 10 common myths," [Online]. Available: https://www.vox.com/cards/transgender-myths-fiction-facts/sexual-orientation-gender-identity-myth.

[12]   B. S. a. L. Badgett, "Beyond Stereotypes: Poverty in the LGBT Community," [Online]. Available: https://williamsinstitute.law.ucla.edu/williams-in-the-news/beyond-stereotypes-poverty-in-the-lgbt-community/.

[13]   Z. Ford, "Housing discrimination against transgender people is even worse than we thought," 2017 3 2017. [Online]. Available: https://thinkprogress.org/trans-housing-discrimination-study-889129c40c1b/.

[14]   "Understanding the Transgender Community," [Online]. Available: https://www.hrc.org/resources/understanding-the-transgender-community.

[15]   "Understanding the Transgender Community," [Online]. Available: https://www.hrc.org/resources/understanding-the-transgender-community.

[16]   R. A. a. E. B. C. D. o. A. a. S. H. C. f. D. C. a. P. Lisa C. Barrios, "School Bullying and Lesbian," 17 October 2016. [Online]. Available: https://www.stopbullying.gov/blog/2016/10/17/school-bullying-and-lesbian-gay-and-bisexual-high-school-students.html.

[17]   S. K. M. M. L. & A. M. (. J. S. E. H. J. L. Rankin, "The Report of the 2015 U.S. Transgender Survey, Chapter 14," Washington, D.C., National Center for Transgender Equality.

[18]   S. K. M. M. L. & A. M. (. J. S. E. H. J. L. Rankin, "The Report of the 2015 U.S. Transgender Survey, Chapter 13," (2016).

[19]   "Human Rights Campaign," 2018.

[20]   "2018 LGBTQ Youth Report, Trans Youth Need Our Support," 2018. [Online]. Available: https://assets2.hrc.org/files/assets/resources/2018-YouthReport-NoVid.pdf?_ga=2.27771068.1880459182.1550096788-1042517524.1532103907.

[21]   R. Dommu, "Out Dot Com," 16 November 2018. [Online]. Available: https://www.out.com/news-opinion/2018/11/16/hrc-publishes-new-data-detailing-how-unsafe-trans-teens-feel-school.

[22]   "2018 LGBTQ Youth Report, When Schools Fail," 2018. [Online]. Available: https://assets2.hrc.org/files/assets/resources/2018-YouthReport-NoVid.pdf?_ga=2.27771068.1880459182.1550096788-1042517524.1532103907.

[23]   H. R. Campaign, "2018 LGBTQ Youth Report, The Burden of Rejection," 2018. [Online]. Available: https://assets2.hrc.org/files/assets/resources/2018-YouthReport-NoVid.pdf?_ga=2.27771068.1880459182.1550096788-1042517524.1532103907.

AFTERWORD

Knowing what being transgender is will be essential for those supporting their loved one. My hope is this book presents an insight into transgender people and what they face. Though there are many negative factors, their transition is worth it. Their loved ones will be happier when they reach their selected congruence. When they supply pronouns you do not recognize, remember they are identifying to you who they are. For a list of common pronouns, look at Appendix Two.

Thank you for giving them the guidance to carry this out. Support is so necessary for every transgender individual. Transgender people appear as a new thing to most people, but the recorded history extends back to the 25th century B.C. Transgender people have likely been around since humanity's creation.

There is hate, violence, bullying, and hateful things directed at LGBTQ people. Become an ally. By giving back you present a better prospect for transgender people's future. Give them a chance at their happiness.

I am proud to announce my third book. It will be a comprehensive history of the LGBTQ community. I will aim at a younger audience of middle and high school youth. It will be a book for LGBTQ people and their loved ones should put on their reading list. Many people throughout history have been transgender or gay.

APPENDIX ONE: DEFINITIONS

Words, phrases, and definitions are forever changing. This book provides a considerable list of definitions. It is far from complete. I have a list of definitions on my website (https://www.SpanningGenderBooks.com). If you do not see a definition in this book, please email me at Info@SpanningGenderBooks.com. I will seek to add it.

Some definitions overlap.

Definitions:

Advocate: — A person working on behalf of a marginalized group. They may deliver information, encourage social equity, and confront prejudice.

Agender: — This term supports many other genders. Agender are people who sense their gender as neutral or no gender. Many agender people are outside the binary (transgender). Agender is a newer term.

AFAB and AMAB: — Acronyms meaning "assigned female/male at birth". (likewise, designated female/male at birth or female/male assigned at birth). No one gets to select their sex at birth. Transgender people use this term over biological male/female.

Affectional orientation: — Correct phrase used instead of sexual orientation.

Ally: — Cisgender and heterosexual people who advocate and support the transgender and LGBQ communities. An individual should not self-identify as an ally but show they are one through their advocacy.

Allyship: — Building relationships based on trust, consistency, and accountability with marginalized individuals and/or groups.

Androgyne/Androgynous/Androgyny: — A person with masculine and feminine physical attributes. Centered on the gender spectrum.

Androsexual / androphilic — Having sexual, romantic, and/or emotional interest to masculinity or males.

Aromantic — Having little to no romantic attraction or interest in romance. Sometimes abbreviated to "aro" (pronounced "arrow").

Asexual — Having little to no sexual attraction or interest in others. Sometimes abbreviated to "ace."

Assigned sex at birth (ASAB): —The sex a doctor claims you are.

Bias incident: — An action aimed to harm and/or intimidate a person based on their demographic background(s). Transgender individual's gender variance leads to prejudice. It applies to marginalized demographics that relate to them.

Bigender: — Relating to individuals classifying themselves as two genders. A person may identify as many genders (two or more genders). This does not include two-spirit. Two-spirit is a term used by native Americans and First Nations. See Two-spirit.

Binary: — Describes the genders female/male or woman/man. Binary genders are the sole genders observed by most of society as legitimate.

Binder/binding — Undergarment used to reduce how an individual's breasts appear. Binding is the measure of wearing a binder. Transgender males use binding to make their chest more masculine.

Biological sex — Referring to the sex a person is born with. They figure this by chromosomes, hormones, and anatomy. Transgender people may relate to this as "assigned sex at birth."

Body Image: — How a person perceives, functions and experiences their body. Communities, families, cultures, media and our perceptions form our views of our body image.

Bottom Surgery: — Affirming surgery. Likewise known as Gender Confirmation Surgery (GCS).

Butch: — This is an identity that leans toward the masculine. It does not reduce this term to masculine lesbians. Associated with masculine queer/lesbian women, it may represent distinct gender identity and/or expression. This does not suggest they identify as a female.

Cisgender — A person born congruent in their designated sex at birth and their gender. Cisgender is the opposite of transgender.

Cisnormativity: — Of the gender binary male/female. There is a presumption being cisgender is correct and transgender is incorrect. This shows dominance over transgender individuals.

Cissexism/genderism: — A system of discrimination, harassment, and segregation. This oppresses those whose gender and/or gender expression falls outside of cisnormativity. This normalizes the view that sex and gender are the same.

Closeted: — A transgender person who realizes they are transgender but has not come out. They may wait for their body characteristics to change.

Coming out — Accepting or coming to terms with your sexuality or gender identity. When someone shares their sexuality or gender identity with others.

Cross-Dressing (also cross-dressing): — The act of dressing and presenting as a different gender. Transvestite, a demeaning term is a former term for a cross-dresser. Drag performers are cross-dressing performers. They take on stylized, exaggerated gender displays. They are not cross-dressers. It does not tie cross-dressing to a person's gender. An individual who has transitioned is not a cross-dresser.

Demigender: — A partial gender identity. They may not be male or female. Demigender people are non-binary.

Designated Sex at Birth (DSAB): — The interpreted sex at birth. The same as assigned sex at birth. Ninety-eight percent of the populace has sex characteristics identifiable as male or female. The other two percent may have ambiguous genitalia, such as intersex people. (These proportions are approximate)

Discrimination: — Unjust or prejudicial treatment of marginalized people. Examples are not allowing transgender people to use the bathroom of their identified gender.

Drag: — Exaggerated, theatrical, and/or performative gender presentation. Used most to refer to cross-dressing *performers* (drag queens and drag kings). Anyone of any gender can drag. This has nothing to do with a person's sex assigned at birth, gender identity or sexual orientation at birth.

Femme: — Femme is an identity that leans toward the feminine. It does not limit this term to feminine lesbians. It can imply "femme up", relating to "woman" up. Although linked with feminine queer/lesbian women, it's used by many to represent distinct gender identity and/or expression. It does not suggest that one identifies as a female.

Fluid: — When connected to gender, a person whose gender moves around and is not stationary.

FTM (female-to-male): — See trans woman/trans man.

Gender Binary: — Where people view gender as male or female. This oppresses anyone who defies their sex assigned at birth.

Gender Dysphoria: — Anxiety and/or discomfort of one's sex assigned at birth being incongruent with their identified gender.

Gender-Expansive: — A person who extends beyond the societal model for gender. Anything beyond male and female. A synonym of gender-variant.

Gender expression — How one reveals their gender through clothing, grooming, disposition, and other aspects. Same as "gender presentation."

Gender Fluid: — A fluctuating or "fluid" gender identity. See fluid.

Gender Identity Disorder/GID: — DSM-III and DSM-IV diagnosis identifying transgender and other gender non-conforming individuals. This term identifies being transgender as a disorder. It may be abhorrent to particular individuals because of what it signifies. The American Psychology Association replaced this term with "gender dysphoria" in the DSM-5. Even though they replaced GID with gender dysphoria, the stigma persists.

Gender-Neutral: — All-inclusive gender quality such as gender-neutral restrooms.

Gender Non-Conforming (GNC): — Gender identity and expression are incongruent with society's norms.

Gender-Normative: — When an individual's gender identity and presentation align with society's norms. Opposite of gender non-conforming.

Gender Outlaw: — Person who does not live by society's gender-normative arrogance.

Gender Presentation: — Outward gender expression of one's internal understanding of their gender. Synonym of gender expression.

Genderqueer: — A person not identifying in the gender binary. Genderqueer encompasses many other gender identities. Those who dislike labels may use this term. Binary and non-binary people may use this term. Genderqueer is neither transgender nor non-binary.

Gender Role: — An appearance or behavior studied by an individual as relevant for their gender. Determined by the current cultural norms.

Gender-variant: — Gender variant is a behavior or gender expression by an individual not matching societal norms. When a person's gender identity and expression are no longer the gender binary. Synonym of gender-expansive.

Hermaphrodite: — Old term for intersex. This is a defamatory term.

Hormone Replacement Therapy (HRT): — Hormones that alter secondary sex characteristics. Not every transgender person will take hormones.

Internalized Oppression: — Members of a marked group get socialized into believing oppressive ideologies of the class they belong to. Many face stereotypes and prejudices from a young age.

Intersex: — Identifying those whose genitalia, chromosomes, and/or hormones do not match normal sequences. Their genitalia may be ambiguous. They may have androgen insensitivity syndrome (AIS) and many other variations. Doctors do surgeries to match the ambiguous genitalia to a perceived gender. This is a mutilation of a baby who has no voice in who they are. Some intersex people identify as transgender. Intersex is as prevalent in society as redheads. (1.4 percent)

In the Closet: — When a person has realized their identity but has not shown it to anybody. Same as closeted.

MTF (male to a female): — See trans woman/trans man.

Misgender: — Attributing a gender to someone who is not the gender. Using incorrect pronouns.

MOGAI: — An acronym standing for "marginalized orientations, gender alignments and intersex orientations, gender alignments and intersex." (LGBTQ replacement)

Mx.: — Gender-neutral salutation used in place of Ms., Mrs., or Mr.

Neutrois: — Non-binary gender identity. Neutrois falls under the genderqueer or transgender umbrellas.

Non-binary: — Umbrella term for all genders other than female/male or woman/man. Not all non-binary people label themselves as transgender and not all transgender people label themselves as non-binary.

Omnigender: — Being of every gender. Used to invalidate the notion of two genders. Synonym for pangender and polygender.

Oppression: — When one group exploits another to their benefit.

Outing — Spontaneous act of discovering the gender identity, affectional attraction or intersex status identity, affectional attraction or intersex status of a person.

Packing: — Wearing a penile prosthesis (called "packers").

Pangender: — Many gender identities, expressions and presentations. Synonym for omnigender and polygender.

Passing/blending/assimilating: — Ability of a transgender person to pass as their identified gender. For transgender individuals, the outcome is to fit in.

PGPs — Preferred gender pronouns. The pronouns an individual adopts.

Polygender: — Many gender identities, expressions and presentations. Synonym for omnigender and pangender.

Pronouns: — Words identifying an individual in the third person. In English and other dialects, it ties them to their gender.

QPOC / QTPOC — Standing for queer people of color and queer and/or transgender people of color.

Queer: — General term for gender and sexual minorities who are not cisgender and/or heterosexual. They continue to use the term queer as a hateful slur. There are LGBTQ people who have reclaimed queer to identify themselves.

Questioning: — Exploring gender expression and identity. This term is an identity for LGBTQ people.

Stealth: — The ability to pass as your gender in most social conditions.

Stereotype: — A fixed assumption applied within a group. i.e. gay men have HIV, or transgender people are confused. This does not allow for individuality.

T: — Short for testosterone.

Third Gender: — Anything beyond the gender binary.

Top Surgery: — For transgender men, this surgery is for the removal of the breasts. This affords more congruency in their gender. For transgender women, this surgery provides breast enhancement.

Trans: — Prefix or an adjective used as an abbreviation of transgender. Trans comes from Latin meaning "across from" or "on the other side of."

Transgender: — When a person's sex characteristics and gender do not match. It represents a multitude of identities under the transgender umbrella.

Transition / transitioning — The measure of transforming your look, name, pronouns, and physical attributes to be congruent with their gender.

Trans-misogyny: — Coined by author Julia Serano this recognizes the intersections of transphobia and misogyny and how a person experiences this as oppression to transgender females.

Transphobia: — Systemic violence against transgender people. Associated with sentiments such as fear, discomfort, distrust or disdain.

Trans Woman/Trans Man: — Trans woman describes someone assigned male at birth identifying as female. Trans man describes someone assigned female at birth identifying as male. They may or may not identify as transgender.

Sometimes transgender women label themselves as male-to-female (also MTF, M2F or trans feminine). Sometimes transgender men identify as female-to-male (also FTM, F2M or trans-masculine). Inquire before identifying someone. Use the term and pronouns preferred by the individual. MTF and FTM can be objectionable.

Two-Spirit: — An umbrella term indexing various indigenous gender identities in North America. Two-spirit may relate to their affectional orientation.

Vaginoplasty; Phalloplasty; Metoidioplasty: — Surgical realignment providing a transgender person's gender and primary sex characteristics to be more congruent. Very few transgender individuals opt for "bottom surgery." There are many reasons for not deciding for surgery, including cost. The subsequent terms are false, abusive, or archaic: sex-change surgery, gender reassignment surgery, gender confirmation surgery, and sex reassignment surgery.

APPENDIX TWO: ACRONYMS USED IN THIS BOOK

Acronym	Meaning
LGBTQ	Lesbian, Gay, Bisexual, Transgender, Queer (or Questioning)
GCS	Gender Confirmation Surgery
HRT	Hormone Replacement Therapy
DSM	Diagnostic and Statistical Manual of Mental Disorders
WPATH	World Professional Association of Transgender Healthcare
FFS	Feminine Facial Surgery
GID	Gender Identity Disorder
DNA	DeoxyriboNucleic Acid
HIV+	Human Immunodeficiency Virus
FTM	Female-to-Male
MTF	Male-to-Female
ASAB	Assigned Sex at Birth
AMAB	Assigned Male at Birth
AFAB	Assigned Female at Birth
AGAB	Assigned Gender at Birth
GNC	Gender Non-Conforming
USTS	United States Transgender Survey
PFLAG	Parents, Families, and Friends of Lesbians and Gays
NPR	National Public Radio
HRC	Human Rights Campaign
GLSEN	Gay, Lesbian & Straight Education Network
DSAB	Designated Sex at Birth
AIS	Androgen Insensitivity Syndrome
MOGAI	Marginalized Orientations, Gender Alignments, and Intersex
QPOC	Queer People of Color
GTPOC	Queer Transgender People of Color
M2F	Male 2 Female
F2M	Female 2 Male

APPENDIX THREE: HORMONE REPLACEMENT THERAPY EFFECTS

Table of medications taken by transgender people to aid in transition – Female to Male		
Medication	Usual dosing	Route of entry
Testosterone		
Cypionate Testosterone enanthate	50- 200 mg/wk 100- 200 mg/10- 14 days	Subcutaneous (shot) intramuscular
Testopel	75 mg/pellet	Transdermal
Testosterone gel (1%)	2.5- 10 g/day	Gel
Testosterone patch	2.5- 7.5 mg/day	patch

Table of medications taken by transgender people to aid in transition – Male to Female		
Medication Route of entry	Usual dosing	Route of entry
Estradiol		
Estradiol	2- 4 mg/day	Oral
Estradiol valerate	5- 30 mg/2 weeks	Parental (subcutaneous, intramuscular
Estradiol	0.1- 0.4 mg/twice weekly	Trandermal
Anti- androgen		
Progesterone	20- 60 mg PO/daily	Oral
Medroxyprogesterone acetate	150 mg/every 3 months	Intramuscular
GnRH agonist (leuprolide)	3.75- 7.5 mg/monthly	Intramuscular
Histrelin	50 mg/12 months	Implanted
Spironolactone	100- 200 mg PO/daily	Oral
Finasteride	1 mg PO/daily	Oral

Note that all dosing amounts in the charts are an approximation. Your health professional will adjust. PO is by mouth.

APPENDIX FOUR: SUPPORT ORGANIZATIONS

Family Equality Council — https://www.familyequality.org/
Address: 475 Park Ave South, Suite 2100M, New York, NY 10016
Phone: 646-880-3005
Fax: 646-880-3011
Family Equality Council's mission: Advance equality for LGBTQ families, and those wishing to form them. Accomplished through building community, changing hearts and minds, and driving policy change.

The GLBT National Help Center — https://www.glbthotline.org/
Email: help@LGBThotline.org
Address: 2261 Market Street, #296, San Francisco, CA 94114
LGBT National Youth Talk line toll-free phone:
1-800-246-PRIDE (1-800-246-7743)
LGBT National Senior Talk line toll-free phone: 1-888-234-7243
Administrative phone: 415-355-0003
GLBT National Help Center, founded in 1996, is an organization providing vital peer-support, community connections, and resource information for people with questions about sexual orientation and/or gender identity.

Human Rights Campaign (HRC) — https://www.hrc.org/
Email: equalitycenter@hrc.org
Phone: (800) 777-4723
Fax: (202) 216-1596
Address: Human Rights Campaign Foundation c/o Equality Center, 1640 Rhode Island Avenue NW, Washington, D.C. 20036
HRC's transgender resources — https://www.glaad.org/transgender/resources — (advocacy)
The Human Rights Campaign envisions an America where it ensures GLBT basic rights and can be open, honest and safe at home, at work, and in the community.

Parents, Family & Friends of Lesbians and Gays (PFLAG) — https://pflag.org/
Email: https://pflag.org/contact-pflag (email)
Address: PFLAG National Office, 1828 L Street, NW, Suite 660, Washington, DC 20036
Phone: (202) 467-8180 — Fax: (202) 467-8194
PFLAG Our Trans Loved Ones (support for families of people who are trans) — https://pflag.org/ourtranslovedones

Gay & Lesbian Advocates & Defenders (GLAD) — https://www.glad.org/
Email: gladlaw@glad.org
Address: 18 Tremont, Suite 950, Boston, MA 02108
Phone: 617-426-1350

Fax: 617-426-3594

Through strategic litigation, public policy advocacy, and education, GLAD works in New England and nationwide to create a society free of discrimination based on gender identity and expression, HIV status, and affectional orientation.

Lambda Legal Defense and Education Fund — https://www.lambdalegal.org/

Address: 120 Wall Street, 19th Floor, New York, NY 10005-3919

Phone: 212-809-8585

Fax: 212-809-0055

Lambda Legal is the oldest and largest national legal civil rights organization. Their mission is to achieve full recognition for the civil rights of lesbians, gay men, bisexuals, transgender people. Also, everyone living with HIV through impact litigation, education, and public policy work.

Lambda Legal does not charge its clients for legal representation or advocacy. They receive no government funding. They depend on contributions from supporters around the country.

National Lesbian and Gay Law Association (NLGLA) — https://lgbtbar.org/

Email: info@lgbtbar.org

Address: 1200 18th Street, NW, Suite 700, Washington, DC 20036

Phone: 202-637-7661

This is an organization of lawyers, judges, and other legal professionals, law students, activists. Also, affiliated lesbian, gay, bisexual, and transgender legal organizations. The NLGLA promotes justice through the legal profession for the LGBTQ+ community.

Transgender Law Center (TLC) — https://transgenderlawcenter.org/

Email: info@transgenderlawcenter.org

Address: PO Box 70976, Oakland, CA 94612-0976

Phone: 510-587-9696

Collect line for inmates & detainees: 510-380-8229

Fax: 510-587-9699

Legal Help: 415-865-0176

TLC changes law, policy, and attitudes so that all people can live in a safe and authentic atmosphere. Also free from discrimination regardless of their gender identity or expression.

Advocates for Informed Choice (AIC) — https://aiclegal.WordPress.com/

Email: info@aiclegal.org

Address: P.O. Box 676, Cotati, CA 94931

Phone: 707-793-1190

AIC uses innovative legal strategies to advocate for the civil rights of children born with variations of reproductive or sexual anatomy.

APPENDIX FIVE: SUPPORT FOR PROFESSIONALS

Gay, Lesbian & Straight Educators Network (GLSEN) — https://www.glsen.org/
Email: info@glsen.org
Address: 110 William Street, 30th Floor, New York, NY 10038
Phone: 212-727-0135
GLSEN creates safe schools for all, regardless of sexual orientation and gender identity/expression. Their dedication provides an environment, programs, and resources that are inclusive and celebratory of diversity, and sensitive to the role of power and privilege in society.

Gay and Lesbian Medical Association (GLMA) — http://www.glma.org/
Email: info@glma.org

Address: 1133 19th Street, NW, Suite 302, Washington, DC 20036

Phone: 202-600-8037 — Fax: 202-478-1500

The GLMA's mission is to ensure equality in healthcare for LGBT individuals and healthcare professionals. They achieve their goals by using the health and medical knowledge of their members. They offer professional education, public policy work, patient education, and referrals, and promote research.

National Gay and Lesbian Chamber of Commerce (NGLCC) — https://www.nglcc.org
Email: info@nglcc.org
Address: 1331 F Street | Suite 900, Washington, D.C. 20004
Phone: 202-234-9181
Fax: 202-234-9185
NGLCC Global is dedicated to advancing the economic empowerment of LGBTI people everywhere.

APPENDIX SIX: WORKPLACE SUPPORT

Out and Equal Workplace Advocates — http://outandequal.org/

Email: hello@outandequal.org

Address: 155 Sansome St, Ste 450, San Francisco, California 94104

Phone: 415-694-6500

Their mission is to "educate and empower organizations, human resource professionals, Employee Resource Groups (ERGs) and individual employees through programs and services resulting in equal policies, opportunities, practices, and benefits in the workplace regardless of sexual orientation, gender identity, expression, or characteristics."

APPENDIX SEVEN: SUPPORT FOR VETERANS

American Veterans for Equal Rights (AVER) — http://aver.us/
info@aver.us
AVER, Inc. — PMB 416 — 15127 Main Street E, Ste 104, Sumner, WA 98390
Phone: 718-849-5665
They are LGBT-founded veterans' advocacy and service organizations. They dedicate their work to the equal and fair treatment of all service members and veterans. Also honoring the service and sacrifices of all service members and veterans.

OutServe-SLDN — https://www.OutServe-SLDN.org/
admin@outserve-sldn.org
Address: 1133 19th St. NW, Washington DC 20036
Phone: 800-538-7418
Educate the community, provide legal services, advocate for authentic transgender service, provide developmental opportunities, support members and local chapters, communicate effectively and work towards equality for all.

APPENDIX EIGHT: SUPPORT FOR THE ELDERLY

Services & Advocacy for Gay, Lesbian, Bisexual & Transgender Elders (SAGE) — Email: https://sagenyc.org/nyc/

Address: 305 Seventh Ave, 15th Floor, New York, NY 10001

Phone: 212-741-2247

Fax: 212-366-1947

SAGE offers innovative services and programs to LGBT older people throughout New York City and nationwide through our affiliate network, SAGENet. From arts and culture to health and wellness, employment help, and much more.

APPENDIX NINE: RESOURCES FOR THE INDIVIDUAL IN CRISIS

The Trevor Project — https://www.thetrevorproject.org/
Email: info@thetrevorproject.org
Address: PO Box 69232, West Hollywood, CA 90069
Phone: 24/7/365 Lifeline — 866-4-U-TREVOR (866-488-7386)
TrevorChat, their online instant messaging option
TrevorText, a text-based support option
The Trevor Project's mission is to end suicide among gay, lesbian, bisexual, transgender, queer & questioning young people. The organization works to fulfill this mission through four strategies:

• Provide crisis counseling to LGBTQ young people thinking of suicide.
• Offer resources, supportive counseling, and a sense of community to LGBTQ young people to reduce the risk they become suicidal.
• Educate young people and adults who interact with young people on LGBTQ-competent suicide prevention, risk detection and response.
• Advocate for laws and policies that will reduce suicide among LGBTQ young people.

The National Suicide Prevention Lifeline — https://suicidepreventionlifeline.org/
Phone: 24/7/365 Lifeline: 800-273-TALK (8255) — Espanol — 888-628-9454, Deaf and Hard of Hearing: 800-799-4889
The National Suicide Prevention Lifeline is a national network of local crisis centers that provides free and confidential emotional support to people in a suicidal crisis or emotional distress 24 hours a day, 7 days a week. They commit to improving crisis services and advancing suicide prevention by empowering individuals, advancing professional best practices, and building awareness.

Trans Lifeline — https://www.translifeline.org/
Email: contact@translifeline.org
Address: 101 Broadway #311, Oakland, CA 94607
Phone: Lifeline USA: 877-565-8860 — Canada: 877-330-6366
Office: 510-771-1417
Trans Lifeline is a national trans-led organization dedicated to improving the quality of trans lives by responding to the critical needs of our community with direct service, material support, advocacy, and education. Our vision is to fight the epidemic of trans suicide and improve the life-outcomes of trans people by facilitating justice-oriented, collective community aid.

The Trevor Project — https://www.thetrevorproject.org/ Email: info@thetrevorproject.org
Address: PO Box 69232 — West Hollywood, CA 90069

APPENDIX TEN: ADVOCACY ORGANIZATIONS

National Center for Transgender Equality (NCTE) (advocacy) — https://transequality.org/

Email: ncte@transequality.org

Address: 1133 19th St NW, Suite 302, Washington D. C. 20036

Phone: 202-642-4542

The National Center for Transgender Equality advocates changing policies and society to increase understanding and acceptance of transgender people. In the nation's capital and throughout the country, NCTE works to replace disrespect, discrimination, and violence with empathy, opportunity, and justice.

Freedom for All Americans (policy and legislative advocacy) —

https://www.freedomforallamericans.org/

Address: 1629 K St NW, Suite 300, Washington, DC 20006

Phone: 202-601-0187

This is a bipartisan campaign to secure full nondiscrimination protections for LGBTQ people nationwide. Their work brings together Republicans and Democrats, businesses large and small, people of faith, and allies from all levels of society to make the case for comprehensive nondiscrimination protections for fair treatment of all.

COLAGE Kids of Trans Community (support for kids of trans parents) —

https://www.colage.org/kot/

Email: colage@colage.org

Address: 3815 S. Othello Street, Suite 100, #310, Seattle, WA 98118

Phone: 828-782-1938

COLAGE unites people with lesbian, gay, bisexual, transgender, and/or queer parents and caregivers into a network of peers. They provide support to nurture and empower all to be skilled, self-confident and leaders in our collective communities.

The Task Force — http://www.thetaskforce.org/

Email: thetaskforce@thetaskforce.org

Address: 1325 Massachusetts Ave. NW, Suite 600, Washington, DC 20005

Phone: 202-393-5177

Fax: 202-393-224

Trans/gender non-conforming justice project

Email: thetaskforce@thetaskforce.org — (advocacy)

The National LGBTQ Task Force advances full freedom, justice, and equality for LGBTQ people.

They are building a future where everyone is free to be themselves in every aspect of their lives. Today, millions of LGBTQ people face barriers in every part of their lives: housing, employment, healthcare, retirement, and basic human rights. These barriers must go. Therefore the Task Force is training and mobilizing millions of activists across our nation.

American Civil Liberties Union (ACLU) (legal services) — https://www.aclu.org/
Address: 125 Broad Street, 18th Floor — New York NY 10004
Phone: 212-549-2500
The ACLU is a non-profit organization whose mission is "to defend and preserve the individual rights and liberties guaranteed to every person by the Constitution and laws of the United States."

National Center for Lesbian Rights - Transgender Law (legal services) — http://www.nclrights.org/our-work/transgender-law/transgender-youth/
Email: Info@NCLRights.org
Address: 870 Market Street, Suite 370, San Francisco, CA 94102
Phone: Legal Help Line—1.800.528.6257 or 415-392-6257
Fax: 415-392-8442
NCLR is a national legal organization committed to advancing the civil and human rights of lesbian, gay, bisexual, and transgender people and their families. They do this through litigation, legislation, policy, and public education. Their community and public education broaden public support for LGBT equality.

TransJustice at the Audre Lorde Project (AIP) (advocacy) — https://alp.org/
Email: jessica@alp.org
Address: 147 West 24th Street, 3rd Floor, New York, NY 10011-1911
Phone: 212-463-0342
Fax: 212-463-0344
ALP is a Lesbian, Gay, Bisexual, Two-Spirit, Trans and Gender Non-Conforming People of Color center for community organizing, focusing on the New York City area. Through mobilization, education, and capacity-building, they work for community wellness and progressive social and economic justice. Committed to struggling across differences, they seek to reflect, represent, and serve our various communities.

APPENDIX ELEVEN: GENERAL INFORMATION WEBSITES

Trans Students Educational Resource (TSER) — http://transstudent.org/

Email: tser@transstudent.org

TSER is a youth-led organization dedicated to transforming the educational environment for trans and gender non-conforming students. They accomplish this through advocacy and empowerment. They also focus on creating a trans-friendly education system. Their mission is to educate the public and teach trans activists on how to be effective organizers. They believe justice for trans and gender-non-conforming youth is contingent on an intersectional framework of activism. Ending oppression is a long-term process achievable through collaborative action.

El/La Para TransLatinas — http://ellaparatranslatinas.yolasite.com/

Email: essie@ellaparatranslatinas.org

Address: 2940 16th St Suite 319, San Francisco, CA 94103

Phone: 415-864-7278

Luchamos por los derechos de las translatinas. Buscamos crear un mundo en el cual nosotras las translatinas sentimos que merecemos protegernos, amarnos y desarrollar nuestras personas. Sobre esta base, nos apoyamos en protegernos de la violencia, el abuso y la enfermedad.

Sylvia Rivera Law Project — https://srlp.org/

Email: info@srlp.org

Address: 147 W 24th St, 5th Floor, New York, NY 10011

Phone: 212-337-8550

Fax: 212-337-1972

The SRLP works to guarantee all people are free to self-determine their gender identity and expression. This is regardless of income or race, and without facing harassment, discrimination, or violence. SRLP is a collective organization founded on the understanding that gender self-determination is intertwined with racial, social and economic justice. They seek to increase the political voice and visibility of low-income people and people of color who are transgender, intersex, or gender non-conforming. SRLP works to improve access to respectful and affirming social, health, and legal services for our communities. They believe that to create meaningful political participation and leadership, transgender people must have access to basic means of survival and safety from violence.

Transcending Boundaries Conference — https://www.transcendingboundaries.org/

Inf0@transcendingboundaries.org

Address: PO Box 30171, Springfield, MA 01103

Transcending Boundaries, Inc. is a 501 (c)(3) non-profit organization that provides education, activism, and support for persons whose sexuality, gender, sex, or relationship style do not fit within conventional categories. The organization serves our ever-evolving communities, including bisexual, pansexual, fluid, queer, transgender, transsexual, genderqueer, intersex, asexual, polyamorous, and kinky persons, and allies and those who prefer not to use labels. Our work includes an annual conference, community outreach, and educational resources.

Transgender Archive — https://www.digitaltransgenderarchive.net/
Email: https://www.digitaltransgenderarchive.net/contact email link
The purpose of the Digital Transgender Archive (DTA) is to increase the accessibility of transgender history by providing an online hub for digitized historical materials, born-digital materials, and information on archival holdings worldwide. Based in Worcester, Massachusetts at the College of the Holy Cross, the DTA is an international collaboration among over fifty colleges, universities, non-profit organizations, public libraries, and private collections. By digitally localizing a wide range of trans-related materials, the DTA expands access to trans history for academics and independent researchers alike to foster education and dialog concerning trans history.

Transgender Foundation of America — http://www.tfahouston.com/
Email: info@tgctr.org
Address: PO Box 542287, Houston, TX 77254
TFA provides homeless services and removes barriers to mental health support through free group therapy, counseling, and vetted referrals. TFA supports community development through supplying free meeting space to groups and by hosting regular events that strengthen ties within the GLBT community.

Transsexual and Transgender Roadmap — https://www.transgendermap.com/
Address: 5419 Hollywood Blvd. # C-142, Los Angeles, CA 90027
Transsexual and Transgender Roadmap is a site offering a large amount of information on figuring out you are transgender and transitioning. The website provides resources and general information.

APPENDIX TWELVE: OTHER INFORMATIONAL WEBSITES

Lynn Conway — http://www.lynnconway.com

Lynn Conway is a transgender professor. She transitioned in 1968, a time when transgender people stayed hidden because of the hate and stigma. They outed her in 1999 through previous work she had accomplished prior to her transition. Lynn's research, along with Carver Mead discovered VLSI Technology used for miniaturizing computers. She founded other technologies along with her storied career. Lynn's website has information on her transition, her work, and her life. There is also information on being transgender and transitioning. Lynn is one of many transgender pioneers that helped the transgender community be where it is today.

Gender Psychology — http://www.genderpsychology.org

Email: madeline@genderpsychology.org

Madeline is a psychology professor who is also transgender (bigender). She has her story on her site about her struggles in finding herself. She has put together some nice material from her perspective as a psychology professor and being transgender. There are many wonderful links on her website.

APPENDIX THIRTEEN: ORGANIZATIONS DENYING REPARATIVE THERAPY

American Academy of Child and Adolescent Psychiatry, Policy Statement:
The American Academy of Child and Adolescent Psychiatry finds no evidence to support the application of any "therapeutic intervention" operating under the premise that a specific sexual orientation, gender identity, and/or gender expression is pathological. Based on the scientific evidence, the AACAP asserts that such "conversion therapies" (or other interventions imposed intending to promote sexual orientation and/or gender as a preferred outcome) lack scientific credibility and clinical utility. There is evidence that such interventions are harmful. As a result, "conversion therapies" should not be part of any behavioral health treatment of children and adolescents

American Academy of Family Physicians,
American Academy of Nursing,
American Association of Sexuality Educators, Counselors, and Therapists,
American Counseling Association,
American Medical Association,
American Medical Student Association,
American Psychoanalytic Association,
The Association of LGBTQ Psychiatrists,
Association of Lesbian, Gay, Bisexual, Transgender Issues in Counseling,
Clinical Social Work Association,
Gay and Lesbian Medical Association,
The Association of Lesbian, Gay, Bisexual, Transgender Addiction Professionals, and their Allies,
&
World Professional Association for Transgender Health

Joint Statement (Draft):

The signatories of this statement share a commitment to protecting the public from the risks and harms of conversion therapy and to ensuring full access to the benefits of ethical, affirmative healthcare for sexual and gender minorities. Given the fact that same-sex desire and behavior and gender-variant identity and expression are not mental disorders, and given the lack of evidence showing that conversion therapy can change sexual orientation or gender identity, and given the strong indications that such change efforts can increase stigma and cause other harms to patients and their families, we urge all healthcare professionals to commit themselves to ensure that: [...]

American Academy of Pediatrics, Policy Statement:
In contrast, "conversion" or "reparative" treatment models are used to prevent children and adolescents from identifying as transgender or to dissuade them from exhibiting gender-diverse

expressions. [...] Reparative approaches have been proven to be not only unsuccessful but also harmful and are outside the mainstream of traditional medical practice.

American Group Psychotherapy Association,
American Mental Health Counselors Association,
Gay and Lesbian Medical Association,
National Association for Children's Behavioral Health, National Association of School Psychologists, &
National Coalition for Mental Health Recovery,

To Whom It May Concern:

There is virtually no credible evidence that any psychotherapy can change a person's sexual orientation, gender identity or expression, and, in fact, conversion efforts pose critical health risks to lesbian, gay, bisexual, and transgender people, including depression, shame, decreased self-esteem, social withdrawal, substance abuse, risky behavior, and suicidality

American Medical Association, Policy H-160.991:
Our AMA: [...] (c) opposes, the use of "reparative" or "conversion" therapy for sexual orientation or gender identity.

American Psychiatric Association, Approved resource document*:
Expert consensus regarding the treatment of adults arrived at after many years of clinical experience. Attempts to engage individuals in psychotherapy to change their gender identity or expression are not considered fruitful by the mental health professionals with the most experience working in this area and legal bans of therapies aimed at changing sexual orientation have recently been extended to therapies aimed at changing gender identity or expression in several U.S. states and Canadian provinces. Psychotherapeutic involvement with adults with GD is primarily used to help clarify their desire for, and commitment to, changes in gender expression and/or somatic treatments to minimize discordance with their experienced gender, and to ensure that they know of and have considered alternatives.

*This document only explicitly opposes conversion or reparative therapy for adults.

American Psychoanalytic Association, Position Statement:
The psychoanalytic technique does not encompass purposeful attempts to "convert," "repair," change or shift an individual's sexual orientation, gender identity or gender expression. Such directed efforts are against fundamental principles of psychoanalytic treatment and often result in substantial psychological pain by reinforcing damaging internalized attitudes.

American Psychological Association & National Association of School Psychologists,
Resolution:
BE IT FURTHER RESOLVED that the American Psychological Association and the National Association of School Psychologists support affirmative interventions with transgender and gender-diverse children and adolescents that encourage self-exploration and self-acceptance rather than trying to shift gender identity and gender expression in any specific direction;

American School Counselor Association, Position statement:
It is not the school counselor's role to change a student's sexual orientation or gender identity. School counselors recognize the profound harm intrinsic to therapies alleging to change an individual's sexual orientation or gender identity [...] and advocate to protect LGBTQ students from this harm.

Association of Christian Counselors,
British Association for Counselling and Psychotherapy,
British Association of Behavioral and Cognitive Psychotherapies,
British Psychoanalytic Council,
British Psychological Society,
College of Sex and Relationship Therapists,
GLADD (The Association of LGBT Doctors and Dentists),
National Counseling Society,
NHS England,
NHS Scotland,
Pink Therapy,
Royal College of General Practitioners, &
UK Council for Psychotherapy,

Memorandum of Understanding:

For this document 'conversion therapy' is an umbrella term for a therapeutic approach, or any model or individual viewpoint that shows an assumption that any sexual orientation or gender identity is inherently preferable to any other, and which attempts to bring about a change of sexual orientation or gender identity or seeks to suppress an individual's expression of sexual orientation or gender identity on that basis. [...] Signatory organizations agree that the practice of conversion therapy, whether in relation to sexual orientation or gender identity, is deemed unethical and potentially harmful.

Australian and New Zealand Professional Association for Transgender Health, Standards of Care:
In the past, psychological practices trying to change a person's gender identity to be more aligned with their sex assigned at birth were used. Such practices, typically known as conversion or reparative therapies, lack efficacy, are deemed unethical and may cause lasting damage to a child or adolescent's social and emotional health and well-being.

Canadian Association of Social Workers & Canadian Association for Social Work Education,

Joint Statement:

Any professional's attempt to alter the gender identity or expression of a young person to align with social norms is unethical and an abuse of power and authority. Specifically, social workers should reject any attempt to prevent a child from growing up to be transgender, transsexual, two-spirit, gay, lesbian, bisexual or queer.

Canadian Professional Association for Transgender Health, Submission in support of Bill 77:

Conversion "therapy" and clinical or "therapeutic" interventions that counsel parents to make their affection, love, and support conditional on restricting a child's gender identity or expression, or that instill shame on children and youth for their gender identity or gender expression are inconsistent with an overwhelming consensus of major mental health organizations have no place.

Canadian Psychiatric Association,

Policy statement:

The CPA opposes the use of reparative or conversion therapy, given that such therapy assumes that LGBTQ identities show a mental disorder and (or) the assumption that the person could and should change their sexual orientation and (or) their gender identity and gender expression.

College of Registered Psychotherapists of Ontario,

Practice Standards:

Seeking to change or direct a person's sexual orientation or gender identity is not 'therapy', are not supported by the profession and does not respect the diversity and dignity of all persons.

International Federation of Social Workers, Statement of Principles:
Social workers must not allow their knowledge and skills to be used for inhumane purposes, such as [...] conversion therapy [...].

Ordre professionel des sexologues du Québec (Professional order of sexologists of Quebec), Public statement (translated):
The Professional order of sexologists of Quebec wishes to inform individuals who might want to receive [conversion or reparative therapy] for themselves or their child [...] that they are prohibited by many regions of the world and by most professional associations in psychology, psychiatry, and medicine and professional orders including the Professional order of sexologists of Quebec, as the present statement evidence.

National Association of Social Workers' National Committee on LGBT Issues,

Position Statement:

The term sexual orientation change efforts (or SOCE) include any practice seeking to change a person's sexual orientation, including, but not limited to, efforts to change behaviors, gender identity, or gender expressions, or to reduce or eliminate sexual or romantic attractions or feelings toward a person of the same gender.

The practice of SOCE violates the very tenets of the social work profession as outlined in the NASW Code of Ethics. [...] The National Committee on LGBT Issues asserts that conversion therapy or SOCE is an infringement of the guiding principles inherent to social worker's ethics and values; a position affirmed by the NASW policy statement on "Lesbian, Gay, and Bisexual Issues" (NASW 2014).

NHS England,
Service Specifications:

Providers will not deliver, promote, or refer individuals to any form of conversion therapy. The practice of conversion therapy is unethical and potentially harmful.

*This document only explicitly opposes conversion or reparative therapy for adults. For a statement including youth, see NHS England's endorsement of the Memorandum of Understanding.

Royal College of Psychiatrists,

Position Statement:

The term 'conversion therapy' has also been used to describe treatments for transgender people that aim to suppress or divert their gender identity — i.e. to make them cisgender — that is only identified with the sex assigned to them at birth. Conversion therapies may draw from treatment principles established for other reasons, for example, psychoanalytic or behavior therapy. They may include barriers to gender-affirming medical and psychological treatments. There is no scientific support for use of treatments in such a way and such applications are widely regarded as unacceptable.

Society for Adolescent Health and Medicine,

Position paper:

Reparative "therapy," which attempts to change one's sexual orientation or gender identity, is inherently coercive and inconsistent with current standards of medical care.

Substance Abuse and Mental Health Services Administration,

Consensus Statement:

Interventions aimed at a fixed outcome, such as gender conformity or heterosexual orientation, including those aimed at changing gender identity, gender expression, and sexual orientation are coercive, can be harmful, and should not be part of behavioral health treatment. Directing the child to be conforming to any gender expression or sexual orientation or directing the parents to place pressure for specific gender expressions, gender identities, and sexual orientations are inappropriate and reinforce harmful gender and sexual orientation stereotypes.

It is clinically inappropriate for behavioral health professionals to have a prescriptive goal related to gender identity, gender expression, or sexual orientation for the ultimate developmental outcome of a child's or adolescent's gender identity or gender expression.

World Professional Association on Transgender Health, Standards of Care:
Treatment aimed at trying to change a person's gender identity and expression to become more congruent with sex assigned at birth has been attempted in the past without success [...], particularly in the long-term [...]. Such treatment is no longer considered ethical.

SPECIAL THANKS TO

My thanks go out to those who influenced me in writing this book. There are many who seen the writer in me and pushed me to start writing and give something back for future LGBTQ generations.

Robert Ruff and Megan Klaeger Ruff – Great friends and advocates. They believe in me and my project. Thanks for your support and encouragement.

Chris Alvarenga – Chris was my inspiration to author books. She reminded me of the seminars I had written. She told me I had a story to tell and to help those needing support and education on being transgender. Chris has also proofed my books for me. I am indebted to her for her friendship and belief in me.

Theresa Doyle – Thank you for proofing this book for me. It is appreciated. Thank you for your friendship.

Jamie McAfee – Thank you for helping by proofing this book. Forever friends.

To all others who have provided me inspiration and input, I am forever indebted to you. Thanks for being in my life.

ABOUT THE AUTHOR

Stephania M. Kanitsch was a Metrologist at the Palo Verde Nuclear Power Plant. She now spends her time authoring books and advocating for the transgender community when she can. Stephania was a board member and vice-president of a non-profit. She found that her passion for the transgender and LGBTQ community came out in the seminars she wrote while at the non-profit. Her home is in the Central Texas Hill Country.

Earlier books by Stephania Kanitsch:

So, you're transgender. Now, what?

So, you're transgender. Now, what? Is my first book. It is written for the person who may be questioning their identity, starting transition, or those who love the transgender person and want to learn about what being transgender is about.

INDEX

H

I

M

O

Oppression

P

R

V

W